The
PIERRE
BOTTINEAU
～ *and the* ～
RED RIVER TRAIL

ESCHIA
BOOKS

Ted Stone

©2013 by Eschia Books Inc.
First printed in 2013 10 9 8 7 6 5 4 3 2 1
Printed in Canada

The Publisher: Eschia Books Inc.

Library and Archives Canada Cataloguing in Publication

Stone, Ted, 1947–
The legend of Pierre Bottineau and the Red River Trail / Ted Stone.

Includes bibliographical references.
ISBN 978-1-926696-22-5

1. Bottineau, Pierre, 1817–1895. 2. Métis—Biography. 3. Pioneers—
Canada, Western—Biography. 4. Red River Trail—History. 5. Frontier
and pioneer life—Canada, Western. I. Title.

FC3213.1.B68S76 2013   971.2'01092   C2012-908201-5

Cover Image: © Digimarc.com
Photo Credits: Every effort has been made to accurately credit the sources of photographs and images. Any errors or omissions should be reported directly to the publisher for correction in future editions. Images courtesy of Alesha Braitenbach (p. 4, map of Red River Trail), Archives of Manitoba (pp. 43, 232); Glenbow Museum (pp. 26, 72, 81, 114, 132, 164, 224, 236), Library and Archives Canada (p. 28), Library of Congress (pp. 171, 205, 227, 229), Minnesota Archives (p. 96), Saskatchewan Archives Board (p. 32, 221), Ted Stone (pp. 246, 252, 254), Toronto Public Library (p. 77).

Produced with the assistance of the Government of Alberta, through the Alberta Multimedia Development Fund

We acknowledge the support of the Canada Council for the Arts, which last year invested $157 million to bring the arts to Canadians throughout the country.

 Canada Council   Conseil des Arts
for the Arts   du Canada

For Marg

———————

I thank everyone who helped me with this project, especially Ann Healy, Michael Bailey, Melanie Thornberg, Kathy van Denderen and staff at the Manitoba Provincial Archives, Société historique de Saint-Boniface Centre du patrimoine and Minnesota Historical Society Archives.

Red River Trail

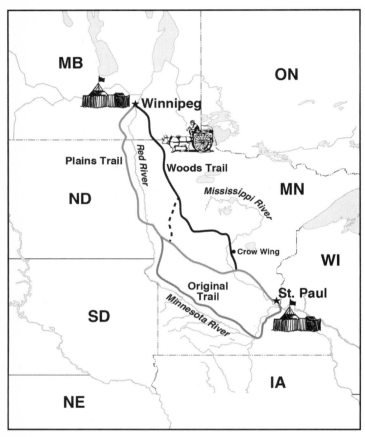

The Red River Trail had two branches leading south from Manitoba. The branch on the west side of the river was often called the Plains Trail; the branch on the east side of the river came to be known as the Woods Trail, though both routes were known as the Red River Trail and had other names as well. The original route led travelers south to the Minnesota River Valley, but the part of the trail along the Minnesota River was abandoned early, and more direct paths to the Mississippi were created on both branches of the trail.

Contents

Introduction

⸺⸺⸺

Describing the Western prairie as a sea of grass is an overused metaphor, but for travelers on the Red River Trail, crossing the open plains in the 19th century, the treed ridges on the far sides of the Red River Valley really did appear like an ocean's distant shoreline. People called the treed ridges the "coast," and the scattered groves of oaks on the open prairie became "islands." It is unsurprising that 8000 years earlier, the forested ridges made up the real shoreline of a huge glacial lake, now known as Lake Agassiz.

I live on a ranch in southern Manitoba, along one of Lake Agassiz's old beach ridges, about two miles east of where a jagged line of oaks and aspens marks a botanical boundary between eastern forest and western prairie. Before Europeans arrived in North America, a squirrel anywhere along this tree line, if it had known the way, could have left the plains and jumped from tree to tree all the way to the Atlantic, without once needing to walk on the ground.

When we moved here, I knew that more than 100 years earlier a branch of the Red River Trail had been somewhere nearby. It was only after the Trans-Canada Trail added a new section just west of our house and named it after an old branch of the former trail that I began to think more seriously about the trail that once connected what is, today, Winnipeg, Manitoba, with St. Paul, Minnesota.

Most of the old Red River Trail is gone now, though disappearing ruts in the prairie can still be found here and there along its old route. At these spots, three parallel lines, almost hidden in the grass, provide evidence of the rough, wooden vehicles—the Red River carts—that once traveled here. The wagons' two large wheels cut the outside ruts into the soil, while the horses and oxen that pulled the jerking, creaking carts up and down the trail made the big rut in the middle.

But the old tracks are disappearing, too, from natural processes and human activity. For the most part, the trail vanished years ago, mostly covered now by fields of grain or sugar beets, or hidden behind encroaching willows and oaks or, perhaps, ripped up and buried by new concrete and asphalt highways. Most people today who live near where the old trail passed know little or nothing about its history.

For a good part of the 18th and 19th centuries, the British territories in western North America were nominally the domain of the Hudson's Bay Company (HBC), but because of the Red River Trail, a smattering of trade between the territories' residents and Americans began as early as 1820. Additional trade with the United States was inevitable as the Red River settlement grew and American fur traders, and then settlers, moved into the upper Mississippi on the American side of the border. In the years after 1820, the Red River Trail became one of the most significant, if least celebrated, frontier trade routes in the North American west.

I drive regularly from my home, near the northern end of what was once the Red River Trail, to the Twin Cities in a few hours, an easy day's drive along a route that would have once taken a horse and rider two weeks or more. The same journey would have taken four or five weeks or longer in a Red River cart. My usual route—following Highway 59 from Manitoba to Detroit Lakes, and then U.S. Highway 10 to St. Paul—corresponds, roughly, to the east branch of the Red River Trail, and I can still see regular reminders of the old trail as I drive.

There are places, especially where pastures on the beach ridges slope down to the open prairies to the west, where the land appears just as it could have looked 150 or 200 years ago. Several of the gravel roads in Marshall County, in northern Minnesota, just west of Highway 59, are marked with old signs that claim the roads to be part of the original Red River Trail. Historical markers from St. Pierre in Manitoba to spots in Kittson County near the Canadian border and Anoka near the Twin Cities, also tell of the old cart path.

I know the old trail passed somewhere close to where I live now, and I often wonder if something might have been dropped along the way—a knife, an arrowhead, a broken musket? It has been more than a century since the trail last went this way, but in the life of the land, it was only recently that Métis traders and teamsters passed by with piebald ponies and noisy wooden carts. Something of the old trail might still be here.

One of the best ways to learn about something is to write about it, and I learned a few things while writing this book. The first was that although historians often call Red River the Selkirk Settlement, as if it were made up of only Selkirk's Scottish colonists, most of the settlers were Métis, the people of both Aboriginal and non-Aboriginal parents who came to define the community in their own way. Looking back on it today, Red River has to be thought of first as a Métis settlement. The Red River Trail, too, was largely the work of the Métis. It was mostly Métis traders who competed against the Hudson's Bay Company, and it was the Métis who built the carts and hauled the furs. And too often it is the Métis' stories we have forgotten.

In telling some of these stories about the Red River Trail, I departed from a traditional, chronological accounting of events and instead divided the book into chapters where stories could be sorted and told on their own merit, based on their particular interest in and contribution to the whole. As a result, sometimes particular historical events simultaneously played roles in more than one of the chapters. In order to keep the reader within the context of time and place, some details have had to be repeated in these instances. Stories of the trail are often tales of individual people, and these narratives have to move ahead in the context of the overall history of the region. One individual's stories became particularly important to this undertaking. As I gathered information about the history surrounding the Red River Trail and the Métis people, I discovered Pierre Bottineau.

The Red River Trail was important in the creation of Minnesota and probably crucial in the development of Manitoba. In my reading, Bottineau's name kept turning up when important events occurred on either side of the border. Time and again it seemed, he would arrive at some historic moment along the Red River Trail. In the days of the trail, Bottineau became known as a guide and scout, but over the course of his life, he earned a living in a dozen different ways. He lived by his wits, schooled in the wilderness of the Red River Country.

For nearly 50 years he guided soldiers, politicians, traders, railroad surveyors, immigrants, hunters and homesteaders. He took cattle and furs down the Red River Trail and trade goods north again. He led a wagon train bound for Montana. Some reports credit him with guiding gold-rush pilgrims to British Columbia, others with helping William Nobles discover the South Pass through the Rocky Mountains to California.

The Boston writer Charles Carleton Coffin described Bottineau, his guide to the Red River country in the 1860s, as "tall and well formed, with features which show both his French and Indian parentage." Coffin's description, in his book *Seat of Empire*, noted that Bottineau was well known to everyone throughout the Northwest, whether American, Canadian or Native.

"He has traversed the vast region of the Northwest in every direction," Coffin wrote in the style of the times. "Like the honey bee, which flies straight from the flower to its hive, over fields, through forests, across ravines or intervening hills, so Pierre Bottineau knows just where to go when out upon the boundless prairie with no landmark to guide him. He is never lost, even in the darkest night or foggiest day."

Another writer had said a few years earlier that Bottineau, presumably when he was still young enough to get lost, did so once in a furious storm. But the mishap created no problem for Bottineau. He simply waited for the weather to pass. By then it was dark, so Bottineau stretched out on the ground, face to the sky, and studied the stars for about half an hour. At the end of that time, he got up and led the party on a direct route to the correct trail.

Years later, Bottineau led a group of homesteaders, including members of his family, up the Red River Trail to the region in northwestern Minnesota where he would live out his life, along the old trail whose days were also coming to an end. Bottineau had been born on the trail just as it came into use, and he died, in old age, only a few years after horse and cart trains on the old trail had faded into memory.

Now and again, some writer would call Bottineau the "Kit Carson of the North," a comparison that paid as much homage to the old Santa Fe Trail frontiersman as the northern guide. Physically, the two men could not have been more different. Carson, despite his remarkable life, was a bantam of a man, while Bottineau stood a stocky six feet tall and weighed over 200 pounds. Both were rare personalities, a breed lost to history, men who vanished with the end of the North American frontier. Both were well known in their time. Both took part in some of the major events of their individual regions; both, though illiterate, spoke several Native languages, plus English and French and, in Carson's case, Spanish as well.

But it serves neither man justice to dwell long on the comparison. Both lived remarkable lives of hardship and adventure. Both took part in some of the incredible tales that grew up around two great frontier trails. Both worked hard and died poor, but they were also as different as the important trails they followed. We know more of Carson's life and legend; more was put on paper while he was still alive, but the tales we know of Bottineau's life create a similarly compelling story along a now almost forgotten trail.

Chapter One

The Blizzard

Late in the winter of 1837, Pierre Bottineau agreed to lead three men from the east, anxious to leave a frontier settlement in what is now Manitoba, down a trail that followed the west side of the Red River of the North.

People called the route the Red River Trail. At the time, the trail was almost unknown outside the region, but for the settlement's people, it had already become a vital link to the outside world. The trail paralleled the Red River for its first 200 miles until, nearing the halfway point, it crossed the Continental Divide between the Arctic and Atlantic watersheds. After that, the original route followed the Minnesota River southeast to its mouth on the Mississippi. An American army post had been built at the confluence of these rivers, and every spring, when ice on the Mississippi melted, steamboats came north from St. Louis.

Bottineau and his three charges, with a dog team to carry supplies, began their journey at La Fourches, or The Forks, the isolated frontier settlement sometimes simply called Red River because it sat on the banks of that river, where Winnipeg is today. The four men stuck to the high ground, in most places only about 25 miles west of the river. Bottineau had already used the route several times in his young life. He had been born 20 years earlier, at a wintering camp near the trail in today's North Dakota where his Ojibwa mother and French Canadian father stayed after an autumn buffalo hunt. In all likelihood, the young Bottineau had been on at least a portion of the trail every year of his life.

As for the three men Bottineau led south, only weeks before they had been part of a small, private army with the goal of promoting revolution among the Pueblo Indians of New Mexico. Organized by a shadowy character named James Dickson, the aspiring army left Buffalo, New York, with 60 men heading for the British Northwest in what was to have been a recruitment drive among the mixed-blood population at Red River. They sailed across the Great Lakes from the east to Sault Ste. Marie in a schooner, oared across Lake Superior and then hiked the rest of the way through the wilderness to Manitoba in what could only be described as a roundabout route to Santa Fe.

But the Hudson's Bay Company (HBC) had no desire to see the Métis of the region playing a role in any army, so it refused to sell Dickson supplies and did everything it could to discourage his plans. A grueling, three-month journey to get to Red River just before Christmas, along with the continuing discomfort of a Manitoba winter, took the steam out of the would-be Native liberators long before temperatures rose high enough for their march to Santa Fe to begin. On top of that, Dickson was unable to convince any of the Métis at Red River to join him.

For the most part, the army's soldiers turned out to be nothing more than a rag-tag assortment of misfits and adventurers. Most of them had deserted before they made it to Red River, so the bizarre plan never really got off the ground. Fleeing

Manitoba ahead of the few who remained, or harassed to leave by the HBC, the three men with Bottineau were trying to cross the 550 or so miles between Red River and the Mississippi in time to catch the first steamboat of the season going south to the civilization of St. Louis.

But the realities of winter on the Red River Trail struck early and often. A series of snowstorms began on the second day of their journey, and the few breaks that occurred in the stormy weather afterward brought nearly unbearable cold. One of the men, apparently with the last name of Parys, failed to bring snowshoes, which left him constantly exhausted in the deep snow and continually lagging far behind the others.

Already in his 50s, Parys had once been a captain in Napoleon's army, but how he became involved in Dickson's Santa Fe scheme is unknown. On the evening of March 16, 1837, Parys fell farther behind on the trail than usual. Bottineau and the two others, the young Martin McLeod, who later rose to prominence with the American Fur Company, and a man named Hayes, made camp early. For half the night they sat around a campfire waiting for the former French captain, but it took Parys until 2:00 AM to reach the camp.

The next morning, with the weather turning deceptively mild, everyone slept in to give Parys a chance to rest. Late in the morning, McLeod began calling for him to get up. When a fight started between the two men, and McLeod pulled out a hunting knife, Bottineau stepped in to break them up.

Afterward, while the other men were still getting ready to leave, Bottineau came across recently made elk tracks in the snow and followed them to hunt fresh meat for supper. He sent his three charges down the trail, bound for the wooded banks of the Wild Rice River that was nearly in sight on the horizon several miles to the south. Unfortunately, before they could reach their destination, a March blizzard blowing in from the north caught everyone by surprise, leaving them exposed on the open prairie. Bottineau had yet to return from his hunting expedition, and the three greenhorns were a few miles from the shelter of the trees along the Wild Rice. Complicating the situation, the trio had drifted far apart on the trail.

The most complete record we have of the storm comes from the diary of Martin McLeod, who wrote that the blizzard was something "no pen could describe." Along with the snow came a fierce wind blowing with ever increasing intensity out of the north, across the flat, frozen landscape. Just as the storm hit, McLeod caught sight of one of his companions, Hayes, drifting away from McLeod's trail several dozen yards behind him. McLeod yelled for Hayes to follow him, but then the snow struck with more fury and he lost sight of the man. McLeod could see nothing but the few feet in front of his face. For all intents and purposes, each of them was alone on the trail.

McLeod first attempted to reach the shelter of a stand of stunted trees he remembered seeing in the distance just before the storm hit, but he got bogged down in a snowdrift that covered what he estimated was a 20-foot deep coulee. Fighting his way out, still in his snowshoes because his hands were too cold to unlace them, McLeod discovered the dogs digging into the snowdrift he was trying to escape. Initially, he dug the dogs out of their holes and made them go with him toward the trees he had seen earlier. Finally, nearly exhausted, he burrowed with the animals into the snow near some small brush along the trail. McLeod makes no mention in his diary of the warmth from the dogs helping him to survive the cold, but the next morning, when Bottineau found him, he was still alive.

As for Bottineau, he had briefly lost his way in the storm after he failed to notice a shift in the direction of the wind. But he soon got his bearings and then managed to build a campsite in the drifting snow. He started a fire and spent a comparatively comfortable night sheltered from the storm. His three companions had not fared as well. McLeod survived his ordeal, but when Bottineau found Parys the next morning, the poor man was stuck in the snow up to his shoulders, so badly frozen he was unable to move. There was no trace of the third man, Hayes, though Bottineau spent half of the next day searching for him. The following spring, however, Hayes' two pistols were found abandoned on the prairie.

Parys was too injured to go on, so the guide built a teepee and left the French soldier with food and firewood while he and McLeod went for help at an American Fur Company post more than 50 miles away at Lake Traverse. McLeod, it was said later, was barely up to the journey and would have never made it in the cold and snow except that, every time he faltered, Bottineau hit him with his rifle butt to keep him moving.

After two hard days on the trail, the men reached the fur post, with Bottineau practically carrying his exhausted companion. The young guide took a short rest and then headed back again with an employee of the fur company, a pair of Indian ponies and a Red River cart to retrieve Parys. By the time they got to where the former French soldier had been left, there was nothing to bring back but a body.

A few weeks later, after recuperating at Lake Traverse, and for a few days more at a trading post at Traverse de Sioux downstream on the Minnesota River, Bottineau and McLeod completed their journey to the Mississippi. Bottineau stayed only a few days before heading back up the trail to Red River, but for years afterward, the tale of the blizzard in 1837 was talked about over and over again when people told stories about the Red River Trail or the exploits of Pierre Bottineau.

Chapter Two

The Trail

In many ways, the Red River Trail resembled the better-known Santa Fe Trail that came into use about the same time. Both trails led from an American frontier community into the territory of another nation. They each brought American commerce to an isolated agricultural settlement and were connected to the fur trade. Both trails, essentially, began to be used in the 1820s and lasted for approximately 50 years, until supplanted by railroads. But the Santa Fe Trail is still celebrated in history and folklore, whereas the Red River Trail, which fostered just as many frontier adventures and a more lucrative commerce, though not so many legendary tales, is largely forgotten.

In 1821, William Becknell, the first American trader to reach New Mexico, arrived in Santa Fe with trade goods from Missouri. The same year, Michael Dousman tried to take 200 head of Missouri cattle up the Red River Trail. But unlike Becknell, who achieved immediate success at Santa Fe, Dousman's cattle drive went amiss. Stopped near Big Stone Lake, on today's Minnesota-South Dakota border, Sioux hunters took to Dousman's cattle as if they were wild buffalo. Dousman could not prevent the Natives from killing his herd. All he could do was watch as the animals, bound for Red River, were slaughtered.

Although Dousman's cattle drive was a bust, he returned the following year with another herd that he took all the way to the Red River country. That success was followed by a series of additional cattle drives on the trail to Red River, but more than livestock ranching was established at Selkirk's Colony with the help of the trail. Grain farming, too, owes its real start to seed brought in from the south.

From the beginning, seed had been scarce at Red River, but following widespread crop failures in 1818 and 1819, almost nothing was left to plant in the spring of 1820. To avoid complete disaster, an expedition from the colony was sent down the trail, traveling all the way to Prairie du Chien, near the mouth of the Wisconsin River on the Mississippi.

Here, the settlers purchased 250 bushels of wheat and returned to the colony on the Red River, poling the grain up the Mississippi and Minnesota rivers in flat-bottomed boats, dragging the vessels across shallow water in the marshes on the Continental Divide and floating with the current down the Red to arrive back at their settlement in early June. The venture was so successful and the wheat grew so well that the primary wheat on the Canadian prairies for decades afterward was known as the Prairie du Chien variety.

Despite these early successes on the trail, trade was hampered for years at Red River partly because the Hudson's Bay Company held a royal charter granting it a monopoly in commerce and sovereignty over its territory. The company insisted that trade in hides and furs, the backbone of the local economy, lay exclusively within its domain. But as powerful as the HBC was, it ultimately held an untenable position.

Its alternative trade and communication routes to the Red River Trail were either north through Hudson Bay and across the North Atlantic to Britain, or if necessary, over an even more arduous eastern path in the canoes of voyageurs through the Great Lakes to Montreal. The problem for the Hudson's Bay Company was that furs, generally, fetched higher prices, and trade goods were cheaper and more numerous, though sometimes poorer in quality, to the south, on the upper Mississippi. It was only a matter of time before the furs and buffalo hides of upstart HBC competitors were smuggled to the Americans. Indeed, trade on the Red River Trail was so advantageous that the great fur company eventually took its own freight up and down the trail instead of using the traditional route to the north. But first, for a few years, the HBC tried to fight the free traders it claimed were really nothing but "smugglers."

In addition to the obvious advantages that trade with the United States offered to Red River residents, an equally compelling force was at work. The Métis made up the majority of the population at Red River. Many had family roots on the fur trade trails to the southeast, and they often had relatives living in northern Michigan, Wisconsin or on the upper Mississippi. Family and fur trade connections linked these people at Red River to places such as Sault Ste. Marie, Mackinac and Prairie du Chien in the United States. For most of the Red River Métis, who looked at all of the northern Great Plains as home, the idea of the invisible 49th parallel representing some sort of barrier to trade or movement seemed almost inconceivable, certainly nothing to take seriously.

Long before the Métis started following the Red River Trail, Native Americans, arriving from the south after the glaciers melted, developed hunting and trading trails through this region. About 10,000 years ago, as the glacial Lake Agassiz grew and receded behind the sporadically disappearing glacier, Aboriginal people established trails along each succeeding shoreline. Like the fur traders and buffalo hunters who came later, the first Aboriginal people preferred the trails on the ridges where the land would have been drier. Later, the descendants of these and other Aboriginal people would come to use some of these same trails.

When Americans began moving into what became Minnesota, the Métis were already there to meet them. And when trade goods started coming up the Mississippi with the Americans, the Métis put the old trails to use, carrying the commerce farther north into British territory. By the 1850s, the cart trails and their commerce had been extended from the Red River Trail west across the prairies of western Canada, all the way to the Rocky Mountains.

Trade on the trail to St. Paul had reached a point where the ox carts often numbered 100 or more. Going south, the wagons were packed high with furs, buffalo hides and sometimes moccasins, pemmican and other goods produced by Métis or Native people. Going north, the carts carried European and American-made trade products, which by then also included farm tools and luxury items.

Some sort of trail going south from the forks of the Red and Assiniboine rivers was used in the fur trade as early as 1812, and even then there were probably two branches, one on each side of the river. The most dependable branch of what became the Red River Trail crossed the open prairie west of the river, through today's North Dakota. It was less vulnerable to bogs and mud holes during rainy seasons than the branch that passed near where I live now on the east side of the river.

The eastern branch of the Red River Trail, which became more widely used after 1844, went by several names: the Woods Trail, the Crow Wing Trail, and the Pembina Trail, among others. It all depended on who was talking and which way they were going. Heading toward Pembina, it was called the Pembina Trail. On the way to Crow Wing, it became the Crow Wing Trail. People called it the Red River Trail only when they were unconcerned about making a distinction between the trail's eastern and western branches, which often joined at some point soon after the western branch crossed the Red on its way to the Mississippi.

There was also a wet, little-used branch of the trail closer to the river on the west side of the Red, usually called the River Trail, but the main route on that side kept as close as practical to the higher ground bordering the Pembina Mountains and the ancient beach ridges that mark the west side of the valley. The ridges there, like the lower rises on the east side of the river, usually provided a drier route for travelers; the creeks were narrower and easier to cross farther upstream from the Red. Even the mosquitoes were fewer in number in the higher country farther west.

When the trail was in use, the western branch was also sometimes called the Ridge Trail or the Plains Trail, descriptive names that noted the contrast between it and the Woods

Trail on the east side. As the western trail approached the headwaters of the Red River at Lake Traverse on the northeastern corner of today's South Dakota, it began to angle southeast above Big Stone Lake, crossing the river and skirting the marshy Continental Divide to the upper reaches of the Minnesota River. From there, in the early days, the trail essentially followed the Minnesota southeast to the Mississippi.

Cutoffs around meanders and connecting links on both sides of the Red River were created and abandoned regularly, used for reasons that varied from personal whims to avoiding conflicts with Native people. In many places, the trail wasn't a set route so much as a hodgepodge of interconnected pathways between two end points woven into the map of what was, for both Britain and the United States, a remote northwestern wilderness.

After they arrived at Big Stone Lake, many of the trail's early travelers built rafts to float down the Minnesota to the Mississippi. Others took to canoes on the river (at that time called the St. Pierre or St. Peter River), but well-defined land routes to Traverse de Sioux and the Mississippi beyond were also used. After a few years, the southern section of the earliest route went out of favor, so that when people talked of the Red River Trail (or the Plains Trail), they usually meant a more direct route between St. Paul and the Red River country. The new route crossed the prairies and lake country of central and northwestern Minnesota, roughly following a path that stayed north of the Minnesota River's watershed.

In 1844, a new branch of the Red River Trail created a more northerly route through Minnesota on the east side of the river. This branch, the one often called the Woods Trail, followed the Mississippi north from St. Paul until it reached the mouth of the Crow Wing River. It then followed that river, and succeeding ones, west into northwestern Minnesota and, eventually, frontier Manitoba. But on this route, too, the trail included a regularly used link south to its other branch.

There seemed to be no end to the choice of routes available for folks on the Red River Trail. Traders could follow the east or the west side of the Red River south from Manitoba, but people could easily switch to the other trail at several places along the way. No matter which branch was initially chosen, the trail always had access to a spider web of ancient Aboriginal trails across the western plains and frontier woodlands of the region, and the trail, for those starting in the north, ended at the Mississippi at what became Minnesota's Twin Cities.

Chapter Three

The Métis

Before there was a Red River Trail, the first Métis were born in the east of Aboriginal mothers and fur-trade fathers. Some came west with the fur companies through the Great Lakes and the Wisconsin River to the Mississippi; others came over the Grand Portage to Lake of the Woods and the Great Plains beyond. By the last half of the 1700s, there were Métis already living in the Red River country.

For the first 20 years of the 1800s, competition between fur companies flourished. Jobs were plentiful, and increasing numbers of Métis living around the Great Lakes were also enticed by the companies to immigrate to the plains. Later, particularly after 1821 when the companies consolidated on the north side of the border into the Hudson's Bay Company, many of the Métis lost their jobs and made what living they could as trappers, traders and buffalo hunters.

The Métis were a diverse group. Some adopted the ways of the white people in the settlements. Others preferred the freedom of the open plains and the life of their Aboriginal cousins. Many were somewhere in between, but no matter where or how they lived, the Métis were tied together by a common heritage, a mix of two cultures.

Most were of French and Aboriginal ancestry, but at the Red River settlement they were also often the offspring of

A Métis home at Red River.

Native mothers and Scottish, Irish or English fathers. Many spoke several languages: French, English and one or more Aboriginal language, as well as Michif, the common patois that was created from a mixture of Cree, Ojibwa and French, with a few Gaelic words thrown into the stew. Few Métis of the time could read or write, but for those who could, the common standard was French. And as the years went on, more and more of the English-speaking Métis families were assimilated into the French-speaking community.

Today, we probably remember the Métis of the plains most for the large, traditional buffalo hunts that, for a few years, underscored the economy at Red River. Often, the Métis followed old trails south, along the initial leg of the Red River Trail, before turning west to look for buffalo near the Turtle Mountains or on the high plains of the Dakotas or even farther west in what became Montana and Saskatchewan.

Hunting buffalo was so important that the Métis, who prized the freedom found on the open plains above almost everything, gave in to the demands of the hunt to become disciplined frontiersmen. As the buffalo became more scarce as the years passed, the annual community hunts had to move farther across the plains to find success. In the competition for buffalo with the Sioux and other enemies, the hunts grew larger as a means of protection. By the 1820s, the organization of the hunts became more formal, with elected leaders such as a president, counselors and several captains. Each captain led 10 soldiers, or lieutenants, who acted as policemen for the rest of the group. The captains also took turns scouting for buffalo herds.

The hunts evolved as the years passed, becoming more disciplined, although punishments for infractions were never harsh. Anyone could go on a hunt: men, women and children. Sometimes a Catholic priest would come along, a practice that tended to impose more rules on the hunters (no hunting on Sundays, for example). Non-Métis who wanted to take part were also welcome, including local whites or visitors who happened to be passing through. Some of the Ojibwa around Red River, known as Saulteaux, also liked to hunt buffalo with the Métis, largely because of the safety that came with their larger numbers.

But everyone had to follow the rules if they wanted to hunt. It was especially important not to run the buffalo before the general order was given, so that as much meat as possible could be taken and everybody would have a fair chance. According to the Red River historian Alexander Ross, who went along on and recorded the summer hunt in 1840, the

Métis left with 1600 people and more than 1200 Red River carts. They rode for 20 days south and west of Pembina before finally sighting buffalo. At the command, more than 400 horseback hunters sprang forward and raced after the quietly grazing animals. Reaching full gallop, the hunters made it to within 400 yards of the herd before the buffalo took flight.

The riders steered their mounts with their legs, leaving their hands free for loading and shooting. They carried spare

Métis hunters tried to ride to the front of a stampeding buffalo herd to shoot the faster-running cows. It would have been easier to shoot the slower bulls, but meat from the cows tasted better.

musket balls in their mouths and powder in their pockets. Hunters and horses dashed into the stampeding buffalo, but for the most part the riders held their fire until they reached the lead animals. It was more dangerous to ride at the head of the stampede, of course, but the best meat came from the cows, which were lighter and faster than the bulls, so ran at the front of the herd.

According to Ross, despite the obvious dangers, only one horse was killed in the 1840 hunt, though two more were injured in falls. None of the Métis died during the hunting, but one rider broke a shoulder when his horse fell and another accidently shot himself in the hand after reloading. Later that summer, or perhaps on another hunt, a man named Louison Valle was out hunting with his son when Louison shot a buffalo. Because the Métis were hunting in Sioux territory, Louison told his son to stay on a small rise on the prairie to keep watch while he set to work skinning the animal.

Unfortunately, a handful of Sioux warriors snuck in from the side. Seeing them too late, Louison yelled for his son to flee just before the father was shot and killed with a flurry of Sioux arrows. The boy, meanwhile, rode for help. Hearing his call, other Métis soon gave chase, overtaking and killing eight of the Sioux, while four others escaped.

In Ross' history of the Red River settlement, he said that during the time he was with the Métis hunters that summer, they killed nearly 1400 animals. The buffalo yielded more than one million pounds of meat, the equivalent, Ross said, of 225 pounds for each of the more than 4000 people who then lived at Red River. Much of that meat would be made into pemmican, the dried staple of the fur trade, and sold to the Hudson's Bay Company.

Pemmican was the standard provision: the dried meat was flailed into a powder, packed in fat and then sealed in a rawhide bag. Sometimes dried berries were added. Well-made pemmican could last for months or even years without spoiling. It could be cooked in several ways, but a dish known as *rubaboo*, made by stirring pemmican in boiling water, while adding salt and a little flour, was standard. Served in cups, along with tea and a basic flour biscuit known as bannock, *rubaboo* was probably the most common meal eaten on the trail. Supper was sometimes more extravagant, with fried pemmican and small chunks of potatoes or an onion when available.

In 1840, the HBC bought 459 bales of pemmican from Métis hunters, with each bale weighing 90 pounds, as well as 150 bales of dried meat, 3500 pounds of fat and 500 buffalo tongues. All of this did not go to the company from this one hunt, but by the same token the HBC was not the only destination for the products of the hunts. Some of the trade, of course, went to American traders, and the Métis also had to keep enough provisions to see themselves and their families through the winter.

Of the two major Métis hunts that took place each year, the summer hunt brought out the most people and killed the most buffalo. Starting sometime in late June or July, the long caravans of ox carts sometimes remained away from the settlement until late in August or September. The fall hunt, on the other hand, usually attracted fewer people, but as the last hunt before winter, a successful hunt was sometimes crucial for survival.

The fall hunts also accounted for the most valuable buffalo hides. At the completion of the fall hunt, many participants dispersed to selected winter camps on the plains where buffalo or other types of game were likely to congregate. Sometimes, these camps were near rivers or on lakes where fishing was also known to be good. In this way, the coldest months could be spent where potential food sources offered additional security against starvation.

For Métis hunters, life on the prairie, with the excitement of the chase and the freedom of the trail, was more than just a way of life; it was, to their minds, the best life possible. There were, of course, other occupations, but much of the Métis population seemed to gravitate toward the nomadic life of the trail and plains. Men who didn't take part in the semiannual community buffalo hunts often engaged in one of the other roving occupations. They freighted York boats for the Hudson's Bay Company, hauling goods from York Factory (the port on Hudson Bay through which company trade passed back and forth between Britain and North America) or pemmican from Red River to Norway House. Métis men from Red River oared the waters of the Saskatchewan and Athabasca rivers in the north and canoe men paddled the old North West Company water route carrying messages between Red River and Montreal. Other Métis became guides, hired hunters, messengers for the fur companies and scouts for the American army or Royal Canadian Mounted Police. Many spent their life on the plains as trappers or traders.

It was also the Métis who took the Red River cart trains south to the upper Mississippi along the Red River

Trail, usually in spring, after there was enough grass growing on the trail for animals to graze. As the cart trains became larger in the 1830s, the Métis organized themselves with the same kind of discipline they displayed on buffalo hunts. The long caravans were divided into brigades, with captains in each brigade elected by their comrades. Small groups of carts were hitched together so that one driver could pilot as many as three, four or five ox-drawn wagons. Each cart might be loaded with as much as 1000 pounds of furs or trade goods.

Just like on the hunts, everyone was welcome to join the cart trains, especially family members. Women, in fact, sometimes drove carts of their own. You could tell the ones driven by women, it was said, because they were painted or otherwise

A Métis family is seen with two Red River carts at a camp on the trail.

decorated, while men's carts appeared strictly of functional design and decoration.

Ideally, the trip to St. Paul could be made in a month or a few days less, but in practice, the time was often greater because of the possibility of all manner of delays and mishaps sure to accompany any journey of such duration in so remote a corner of the world. Still, an essential rhythm developed around life on the Red River Trail. After a day on the trail, there might be time for fiddle playing and some dancing or perhaps games, before turning in for the night.

While the expanding trade on the Red River Trail developed slowly, from the beginning, the Métis used it most. Red River carts had been a conveyance of the Métis for at least a generation before the trail came into general use. The design was much like the vehicles common in Quebec at the time, that were based on traditional European carts. The Red River carts were similar in appearance to the Spanish carts that went back and forth on the Royal Road between Chihuahua and Santa Fe in the years before and after the American leg of the Santa Fe Trail opened.

Red River carts were pulled by oxen or Indian ponies, the horses raised by Native people and developed from the first Spanish horses brought to North America. Later, mules pulled some of the carts, but no matter which animal was used, the carts could carry several times as much weight as a horse alone.

No metal springs were available to absorb any of the shock of rocks and ruts along the way, so the ride would have been uncomfortable. The driver often preferred to take the reins and walk alongside the wagon rather than ride. Any passenger would almost always sit on the floor at the front of the cart, directly behind the horse. Anyone sitting in any other position, according to legend, risked being pitched into the air at the first serious bump in the road.

The first known written account of the carts were in the journals of the North West Company's Alexander Henry at the turn of the 19th century. He wrote of wheels sliced from logs, but long before the Red River Trail to the upper Mississippi came into regular use, the wooden wheels included spokes, often with tire-like buffalo-skin rims to help hold the assembly together. The two wide-rimmed wheels were at least five-feet high by this time, and they had a markedly concave shape to the outside to add stability to the cart. If a pony spooked and stampeded, the carts rarely flipped over.

But the wooden wheels rubbed constantly against the wooden axles, with no mitigating benefits of petroleum-based lubricants. The wood-against-wood squealing from a long train of carts was so loud, it was said, that the trains could be heard two or three miles away. Grease was not used because it would either cake and dry with dirt from the trail, wearing away the wood where wheel and axle met as if by sandpaper, or it would clog and harden until the vehicle became immobile.

Without grease, the noise from the carts was so loud that drivers would occasionally resort to non-petroleum relief. Stopping in marshy areas to catch frogs, they would stuff the amphibians between axle and wheels to bring short-term relief from the noise. Some Native people, only partly in wit, said that the noise from the carts was so loud it drove the bison away.

The carts were ingenious devices, made entirely of wood and leather. If an axle broke, which could happen four or five times during a trip, it was a relatively simple matter to make another axle from an appropriate aspen or oak log. Even when metal parts became more readily available, the Métis continued to use leather and wood, material that could be easily found on the trail.

The cart trains grew longer as commerce on the trail increased and as the Red River settlement grew. The largest caravans grew from a few dozen carts at the beginning of the 1830s to 100 and more by the 1840s. More and more independent traders went into business in numbers corresponding with the rising population at the settlement, but trade on the trail wasn't restricted to dedicated traders. Anyone at Red River could load up a cart or two with furs to take south to a trading post on the American side of the line or all of the way to the upper Mississippi if they took the notion.

After the HBC finally gave up trying to enforce its prohibition against trading south of the border, and Pembina became less important to the trade in the 1850s, larger cart trains were assembled at Red River. The more carts in the train, the safer the drivers felt from the calamities of the trail, particularly attacks by roving bands of Sioux.

By the 1850s, it was common to see 200 Red River carts along the route between Winnipeg and St. Paul, virtually all of them with Métis drivers. Through the 1860s and '70s, the number of carts making the trip south each year climbed past 1000 and then 2000. One estimate has 3000 carts passing south through Pembina in the spring and summer of 1870.

On the Great Plains, the Métis became so identified with the Red River carts that, in the sign language used by Native people across the West, the symbol for "Métis" was the circle motion of two hands spinning next to each other, imitating the wheels of a wagon, followed immediately by the speaker signing a finger-point to his head with his right hand and then drawing his hand down the side of his chest to indicate a man. To the plains Natives, a Métis was indeed a half-breed—half man and half wagon.

The Métis often called themselves the *Bois-Brules*, or scorched wood, in reference to their skin color, which ranged between the light and dark of their parents and grandparents. Their character was also said to be similar to that of scorched wood, which hardened and became stronger just like the people who drew strength from each culture, white and Aboriginal. But the Métis could as easily have called themselves the *gens libre*, or the "free men" of the plains. The term first developed as a name to distinguish between the Canadian *engages* who worked for the fur companies, and the *gens libre* who came west as company employees and worked independently after their contracts with the company were completed.

These *gens libre* were no longer beholden to any fur company. For the most part, as the free men of the plains, they shared the prairie with the Métis hunters who made their living across the plains, mountains and forests of the North American West. For these folks and, usually, their Métis families, to be called the "free men of the plains" seemed especially apt, and the term *gens libre* became a descriptive designation for the Métis, generally. It certainly highlighted their approach to life on the Western prairies in the mid-1800s.

The Métis saw themselves as having a special bond to the land, and the freedom that came with it. They, like their Native ancestors, were born on the land and held an honest, more worthy title to it than the Hudson's Bay Company with its English Charter to show sovereignty. The company had a piece of paper, but the Métis had inherited the land as a natural birthright from their Aboriginal mothers. By the 1830s, these rough, fun-loving plainsmen would no more listen to what the Hudson's Bay Company said about who they could trade with than they would American soldiers who would one day tell them they had to live on one side of the international boundary or the other.

Following such senseless rules played no part in the cultural heritage of the Métis. Like others who lived on the Great Plains before there were cities or fences, the Métis felt, above all, free. They had little material wealth, but they did what they pleased. Where they lived or shot buffalo, or who they traded with, was nobody's business but their own.

Chapter Four

Red River

P ierre Bottineau was born near the Red River Trail about 50 miles south of what became the international boundary. His birth is said to have taken place on New Year's Day in 1817, but the date, even the place, could be imprecise. Bottineau's parents, Charles Joseph Bottineau and Marguerite Ahdik Songab (Clear Sky), were thought to winter camp along the Turtle River, hunting, fishing and trying to survive the cold months until spring. Neither parent could read or write, and no official account of Bottineau's arrival would have been made at the time. A Hudson's Bay Company post was nearby, but it's unlikely that anybody there would have written down information about a Native woman giving birth in the vicinity.

Even back at Red River, the settlement founded just four years earlier by Thomas Douglas, the 5th Earl of Selkirk, there was as yet no priest or protestant missionary to register Bottineau's arrival. Any official record made of the birth would have likely come sometime after the first priests arrived more than a year later. Perhaps, at some point when the family was back at the settlement, an approximation of his birthday and those of other children in the household might have been told to a new priest. Bottineau could have been given an official birth date in these earliest of records, but even if that documentation once existed, it probably burned when fire destroyed St. Boniface Cathedral at Red River in 1860. As a consequence, we're left to surmise the details of his birth, with only a few historical accounts and census records made long after the event, some of which are contradictory.

At the time of Bottineau's arrival, nobody knew if the place on the trail where he was likely born was in American or British territory. Both countries claimed the upper reaches of the Red River, but few citizens of either country lived there. And for the most part, those who did, would have carried British passports, or, like Bottineau's father and other French-speaking Canadians, held loose but vaguely British sympathies.

In 1818, American and British negotiators finally settled on a boundary across the open plains at the 49th parallel, making Bottineau a potential American, born within the new borders of the United States. But Bottineau would have been able to claim citizenship in either nation. Like many other people in the region, he had Canadian roots and spent his formative years in and around the isolated British outpost at the forks of the Red and Assiniboine rivers. Far from the Canadian colonies, and almost as far from the new American states on the west side of the Appalachians as well, the Red River country lay surrounded by wilderness, at the northern end of the Red River Trail.

The little settlement was unimpressive when the Bottineau family returned to it in the spring of 1817. Its lonely log huts—many with thatched roofs, others still under construction—were spread out along the Red River, just north of a small stockade called Fort Douglas, but dwellings dribbled along upstream and downstream on the shores of both the Red and Assiniboine rivers. The fort had been built on the Red, not far from the mouth of the Assiniboine, to serve as settlement headquarters in what was, in reality, a hodgepodge community. The settlers consisted of Scottish, English, French Canadian and Métis fur traders, along with Ojibwa, Cree and additional Métis who occasionally camped nearby or at other times followed the nomadic lifestyle of their Aboriginal ancestors.

There were also more than 200 new farmers, mostly Scottish, busy building their tiny cabins and farms along the Red for the second time, trying to create a primitive agricultural economy in the Red River country. It was a forbidding task they came to largely because they saw no suitable alternative.

Only a year earlier, in 1816, these same Scottish settlers had fled the tiny Red River colony, chased away by Métis supporters of the North West Company who killed 21 of their number in what the Scots called a massacre but which the Métis dubbed the Battle of Seven Oaks. The Scottish settlers had come to Red River as part of a scheme cooked up by Thomas Douglas to develop an agricultural community of Scottish Highlanders on the North American plains.

Douglas was a major stockholder in the Hudson's Bay Company, and he intended to develop a source of agricultural goods for the company and at the same time resettle former Highland sharecroppers who had been kicked off their ancient homesteads in Scotland. His idea, on one level, was a gigantic charitable undertaking, but it was underpinned with a promise, or at least a reasonable expectation, of benefit for the venerable fur company as well. Douglas reasoned that successful

Scottish farmers in the area might bolster British claims to territory reaching as far south as today's South Dakota.

But from the time the first settlers arrived at the forks of the Red and Assiniboine rivers in 1812, Selkirk's immigrants tilled their fields in almost unrelieved misery and a continual series of defeats. In addition, the new settlers were thrown into the center of a bitter fur-trade war between the Hudson's Bay Company and the Montreal-based North West Company (NWC). In some ways, the Bottineau family had been in the middle of Red River's turmoil from the beginning. Charles Bottineau had worked for the North West Company for more than a decade after coming into the Red River country from Quebec in the 1790s, but by the time Selkirk's first settlers started to arrive, he had fulfilled his contractual obligations to that company and had taken to an independent way of life.

Today's Winnipeg shows little evidence of the city's fur-trading past. There's no museum of the fur trade or much commercial carryover left from the old fur-trade economy. In the early years of the 19th century, however, the forks of the Red and Assiniboine rivers, in the heart of today's downtown Winnipeg, stood at the crossroads of the North American fur country. Here, Hudson's Bay men could find their way north from the plains, on lakes and rivers, all the way to York Factory.

The men of the NWC, on the other hand, brought trade goods to and through the Red River country from Lower Canada by way of the Great Lakes and Lake of the Woods. From Red River, they fanned out every summer on canoe routes leading west to the Rocky Mountains and north almost to the arctic coast. The Forks was also the funneling point for carrying furs from all over the northwest back to Quebec. A few NWC employees also reached the Red via Mackinaw Island and river routes to the upper Mississippi. In addition, Manitoba's central location offered comparatively easy access to the Missouri River fur country and the Rocky Mountains to the southwest.

For the NWC and its employees, the idea of farmers moving into the Red River country to furnish provisions for the Hudson's Bay Company held no appeal. Some of the employees of the HBC also worried that settlers in the fur country would do more harm than good. In 1815, the NWC enticed more than 100 of Selkirk's settlers to leave the colony, offering them free transportation east to Lower Canada with the promise of help to get settled once they arrived. As soon as this group of settlers abandoned the community, the company set itself to fermenting further ill will between its employees and the settlers who remained.

The NWC was particularly successful in this effort with the Métis, claiming that Selkirk's farmers were there to take land that should belong to the Métis. The company ordered many of its Métis employees and some of their French Canadian fathers to harass the settlers. Directed by company officers, the Métis burned cabins and crops until almost all the Selkirk settlers in the colony fled to the north shore of Lake Winnipeg. Only at the end of the summer of 1815, acting on the urging of a Hudson's Bay Company officer, did the settlers finally agree to return to the community.

By the spring of 1816, tensions between the two fur companies peaked, with Métis from the North West Company

Cuthbert Grant led the Métis in the Battle of Seven Oaks and remained a Métis leader until his death in 1854.

raiding a Hudson's Bay post on the upper Assiniboine River and Robert Semple, the governor of the Selkirk colony, ordering the razing of Fort Gibraltar, the North West Company post at Red River. When a band of Métis under the command of Cuthbert Grant was spotted on the prairie at a place known as Seven Oaks, not far from Fort Douglas, Semple took 25 men and went out to meet them.

No one really knows who is to blame for the tragedy that followed—Semple's ragtag platoon of volunteer foot soldiers or Grant's mounted Métis. At one point, Semple evidently flew into a rage and grabbed a Métis' gun. One of the Métis shot the governor in the hip, which led to others shooting, and the Battle of Seven Oaks ensued. When the shooting ended, Semple and most of his men were dead.

Reports are inconclusive about how the Métis fared in this skirmish. One Métis man may have been killed, or possibly the man was only wounded, but either way, the area around Fort Douglas fell once more to the control of the North West Company. Selkirk's remaining Scottish settlers fled for the second year in a row to Hudson Bay posts on Lake Winnipeg, where they spent a miserable winter huddled together with little food and less hope.

But the next year, 1817, brought a new beginning for the little settlement on the Red River. Thomas Douglas had been on his way west through the Great Lakes when word came of the deadly Battle of Seven Oaks, and he was with a platoon of about 100 foreign mercenaries, men who had previously served in the British Army, in what was known as the De Meuron Brigade during the War of 1812. The former De Meurons were mostly German-speaking Swiss, but they included a smattering of Poles and other Europeans, and Douglas had hired them to come with him before he left for the Red River country.

After hearing what happened at Seven Oaks, Douglas led his new soldiers to the head of Lake Superior to capture the North West Company's undefended Fort William. He arrested company officers, charged them with promoting the attack on his settlers and sent the men back to Lower Canada to stand trial. He also sent soldiers across the American border where, without legal authority, they sacked an American fur post operated by the same North West Company officers he had already sent back to Lower Canada.

With Fort William under his control, Douglas stayed for the winter, secure on the shore of Lake Superior where North West Company provisions could be counted on to sustain his army through the cold months ahead. He waited until spring to push on to Fort Douglas, where food might be scarce for 100 additional men. Douglas sent a small detachment of his troops on to Red River where, in early 1817, they retook Fort Douglas in the middle of the night from a group of surprised North West Company defenders who gave up Fort Gibraltar without firing a single shot.

In the spring of 1817, when the Bottineau family came back to the settlement, the Selkirk settlers also returned from the shores of Lake Winnipeg, with Douglas himself showing up soon afterward. While he was there, Douglas promised the settlers help in securing the future of their settlement. He said the De Meurons would stay as a local militia to protect the colony, and like the settlers, they would build homes and farms on the Red, near the mouth of the Seine River, just across the river from Fort Douglas. Seed and livestock would be brought to the settlement. A Gaelic-speaking Presbyterian minister was promised to the frontier community.

The North Westers knew that an established farming community on the Red River would spell trouble for them. If it was successful, such a community would feed employees of the Hudson's Bay Company and allow the company to extend its operations further into the lucrative Athabasca fur trade to the northwest. Almost as seriously as the increase in competition, company officers worried that the settlement might draw a significant number of the North West Company's own employees into the new community. Some of those who had completed their contractual arrangements with the NWC might actually settle in the colony with the Selkirk immigrants. Several of the Canadians, in fact, had expressed an interest in buying their own land in the settlement almost immediately after the first settlers arrived.

The North West Company tried to convince its Quebec-born former employees to resent the settlers, but it had a harder time doing so than it did with the employees still on the payroll. Initially, the Métis were most easily convinced to resent the settlers with patriotic calls to protect what they thought of as a special birth right to the land, owed to them as Native inhabitants of the West. Former employees were not so easily moved.

For the North West Company, Charles Bottineau seemed to be one of the most intransigent. He was one of two French Canadians who sold garden produce to the settlers in 1812 almost as soon as they arrived at Red River. The irony in this act, of course, is that history books give the Selkirk settlers credit for introducing agriculture to western Canada, even though they bought crops from two Métis families when they arrived.

Later, Charles Bottineau and others hunted buffalo to sell to the settlers. Then, as the conflict escalated and the North West Company called on him to help set fire to the Hudson's Bay Company fort at Pembina, Bottineau left on a hunting trip to avoid carrying out the orders. When he returned, the North West Company arrested him for disobedience, though he was soon released and the charges dropped.

Once again, during the winter of 1815–16, Charles Bottineau apparently sold buffalo meat to some of the settlers, and the North West Company arrested him a second time. But because Bottineau was a man of some reputation among the First Nations and Métis, that charge was dropped, too.

None of this is to say that Charles Bottineau was in the pocket of the Hudson's Bay Company. His was one of the loudest voices to complain when an HBC injunction was issued that tried to prevent buffalo hunting from horses close to the settlement. But once the prohibition was retracted, Bottineau again became one of the major providers of meat for the settlers. And in 1816, before the battle at Seven Oaks, he went to Governor Robert Semple at Fort Douglas to warn him of the ill intentions of some of the Métis.

When Thomas Douglas left the Red River Settlement at the end of the summer in 1817, he rode horseback south along the Red River, down a route already becoming known as the Red River Trail. Douglas' guide for the journey was Robert Dickson, a prominent independent trader in the upper Mississippi country. Dickson was a pioneer fur trader on the upper Red River, but over the years he had worked for both American and British fur companies, including the Hudson's Bay Company.

When Douglas and Dickson reached the Minnesota River Valley, they traded their horses for canoes and made their way to Prairie du Chien, Wisconsin. At the time, this small settlement made up primarily of Métis as well as a few French Canadians was the most northerly American community on the Mississippi. From Prairie du Chien, Douglas continued to the eastern United States.

But rather than head directly back to Montreal and then Britain, Douglas stopped first in Maryland, near Washington, where he wrote a letter to the American Secretary of State, John Quincy Adams. Douglas saw the obvious potential for developing trade over the Red River route he had just followed and he touted the benefits of trade between his colony and the United States, urging Adams to lift any restrictions that might be a barrier to that trade.

Douglas' desire to secure commerce between his colony and the American Midwest, however, came with some conflicting emotions. He was anxious for the colony to succeed, but he tended toward an emotional anti-Americanism, sometimes blamed on a childhood trauma caused by the American naval hero John Paul Jones.

Jones had been born near the Douglas estate in Scotland. Although he had only circumstantial evidence to support it, he grew up believing he was the illegitimate son of Thomas' father, Dunbar Hamilton Douglas. All his life, the American Revolutionary War hero thought, perhaps correctly, that the Douglas family had deliberately ignored his birth. In 1778, as a captain in the Continental Navy, Jones was sent to harass British shipping and, if possible, kidnap someone of importance whose freedom could be traded to the British for American prisoners. Jones immediately decided on Thomas' father, who was, at the time, the 4th Earl of Selkirk.

After he sailed into the harbor near the Douglas estate, Jones' plan went awry. First, he decided to stay with his ship and send a small party of men to get the earl. But when the men arrived at the mansion, the elder Douglas wasn't home.

Never mind, said the leader of the delegation, we'll take the boy instead. The pronouncement left a profound scar on the seven-year-old future earl, even though Lady Selkirk immediately squelched the idea. Jones' men got away with only the family silver, but the event left Thomas Douglas with a severe distaste for Americans.

Douglas evidently suspended that distaste for anyone who might help him stimulate commerce along the Red River Trail, making a strong pitch to Adams to promote trade there. But despite the earl's plea, Adams wasn't particularly interested and was distrustful of Douglas' connection to the Hudson's Bay Company. There wasn't enough going on in the Red River Settlement that was of value to the United States at that time, and significant American trade on the Red River Trail was still a decade or more away.

In 1818, Great Britain and the United States agreed to an international boundary spanning the Great Plains at the 49th parallel. Along the Red River, the Hudson's Bay Company continued to trade far south of the new international boundary well into the 1820s. After that, the company was forced to retreat north of the border, at least officially, and other traders and companies moved in to take advantage of the HBC's absence. Even so, the company maintained "independent" traders who ranged south of the border to bring American furs north. Soon, however, protecting Canadian furs from disappearing down the Red River Trail to the Americans became the more important issue for the company.

By then, just like the newly forming trail, the settlement at Red River began to take on a more lasting presence.

And despite a steady stream of hardships and setbacks, it began to grow. Several French Canadian families, along with two Catholic priests, arrived at Red River from the east in 1818, over the traditional water route through the Great Lakes. More families came from Quebec in 1819 and 1820, and most of the new arrivals took part in at least some form of subsistence farming. Thomas Douglas, now back in Europe, died in 1820, leaving a colonial legacy in North America but no further help beyond what had already been started for the struggling settlers.

Another group of Selkirk immigrants, arranged for before Douglas' death, arrived in 1821. Agriculture, like the colony itself, was still tenuous, and more setbacks were yet to come, but within a few years, farming and ranching became at least marginally successful and permanently established at Red River.

Chapter Five

The Upper Mississippi

Immediately after the 1818 treaty established an international boundary 60 miles south of Red River, the United States laid claim to North America as far north as the 49th parallel, but only on paper. In the upper Mississippi and Red River regions, there had never been any lasting evidence of an American presence north of Prairie du Chien. As for the fur trade, the Hudson's Bay Company, along with the declining North West Company, still dominated everything in the region. Even on the Mississippi, itself, nominally independent traders were often working for or with the North West Company.

Apart from a couple of aborted incursions during the War of 1812, the only major attempt at an official American presence on the upper Mississippi was in 1805 when a young U.S. Army lieutenant named Zebulon Pike came north exploring the upper reaches of the Mississippi. It had been only a year and a half since control of Louisiana Territory had been passed to the United States from France when Pike arrived. Although much of the region was outside the boundaries of the new territory, the sale solidified United States claims to what was, at the time, the far northwest. By the time Pike left the region to return to St. Louis and then begin his exploration of the southern Rocky Mountains, where he discovered Pike's Peak and some of what became the Santa Fe Trail, he determined that the source of the Mississippi, and the probable limits of American territory, lay at Cass Lake, near today's Bemidji, Minnesota. As things turned out, it was a notion that was only a little short of the river's actual headwaters at Lake Itasca.

But Pike also made a deal with the Sioux of the region to allow the American government to build a fort on the Mississippi at the mouth of the Minnesota River. Although an island was given Pike's name, the American government otherwise seemed to completely ignore the region for another dozen years, along with Pike's advice to build a fort there.

Then, the same year Thomas Douglas followed what became the Red River Trail to the Mississippi, Major Stephen H. Long ventured north on a second American exploratory expedition to the region. Long, like Pike before him, recommended the establishment of a military post at the mouth of the Minnesota River, on the promontory overlooking Pike's Island from the north. The government approved Long's recommendations, partly in an attempt to keep peace between the Sioux and Ojibwa of the region, but mostly as a means to boost American sovereignty in a region that had been generally hostile to it. The fact that only a couple of marshy miles separated the headwaters of the Minnesota from the headwaters of the Red River and a route to and from Rupert's Land in what became western Canada must have also figured prominently in the calculations.

Still, it would be two years after Long's visit before construction of a permanent fort at the mouth of the Minnesota would get started, and another five years before Fort Snelling would be completed. Lieutenant Colonel Henry Leavenworth arrived at the confluence of the two rivers in

August 1819. He initially built a temporary post on the bottomlands close to the river, constructing a wooden stockade and nearly 50 buildings. The temporary fort included barracks for the post's more than 200 soldiers, plus officers' quarters, with facilities for the families of the married among them.

While most of the officers and their families, living in the make-do shelters, survived the winter in good health, the enlisted men had a harder time in the swampy lowlands along the river. At least 40 soldiers died before the spring of 1820, when Leavenworth abandoned the camp and moved his army to higher ground. For most of the summer, Leavenworth delayed choosing a permanent location for the new fort. Finally, he decided to build it at a spot a couple hundred yards removed from the edge of the promontory where both Pike and Long had said it should go.

Fortunately, Colonel Josiah Snelling arrived from the south before work could begin. Snelling had orders to replace the dawdling commander. Unlike Leavenworth, once he assumed command, Snelling got down to business. He immediately moved the site for the fort back to the promontory overlooking the Mississippi above Pike's Island, and he began work on what he quickly determined would be a stone fortress. By the time General Winfield Scott came north to inspect the new facility in 1824 and name it Fort Snelling, the frontier stockade was the most imposing army post in the American West.

Now a National Historic Site, the diamond-shaped fortress, with sides roughly 400 feet long, rose high over both the Mississippi and Minnesota rivers. The exterior walls were 2 feet thick and 10 feet tall. A half-circle battery commanded traffic on both rivers, and a three-story hexagonal tower with musket loopholes and a canon mounted at the top provided additional firepower above the Minnesota.

Snelling's most important, and most lasting, accomplishment, however, was to establish a permanent American presence in the region. Fort Snelling, at the confluence of the Minnesota and Mississippi rivers, brought more than soldiers north. Because of the fort's location, government agents, licensed fur traders, a few settlers and the occasional tourist came to the new fort on the upper Mississippi. It was because of the fort that the region around it became American in spirit as well as on paper.

John Jacob Astor's American Fur Company became the most immediate beneficiary of the new American presence. The company built a trading post just across the Minnesota from Fort Snelling, at what became the town of Mendota. Business for the fur company was helped somewhat by an American law that excluded foreign traders from operating in the United States. Although the law certainly applied to the Hudson's Bay Company, individuals working in the fur trade ignored the border for the most part, working with the British company one year and the American company, or as independent traders, the next. This was true for Americans as well as Canadians, but most of the employees of the fur trade on both sides of the border in the early years of the 19th century had British or Canadian roots.

The first agricultural settlers to arrive in the upper Mississippi in the early 1820s were immigrants from Red River, at the northern end of the Red River Trail, and they started coming before Snelling finished building his stockade. Because the Sioux had ceded no other land in the region for settlement, the post commander allowed the new immigrants to build homes on the military reservation. These settlers, mostly De Meurons and Métis, turned out to be only the first in a long line of refugees to head down the trail from Red River to Minnesota. Two years after the initial settlers arrived, more immigrants came.

The new immigrants, some French- and some German-speaking Swiss, had been brought to Selkirk's colony in 1821 in the hope of making life at Red River more agreeable for their fellow countrymen, the De Meurons, but most of the new settlers turned out to be no more suited for frontier life in Manitoba than the retired soldiers. The majority had been village people in Europe, storekeepers and craftsmen. They knew little of rural life, let alone the hardships of a harsh North American frontier. And when they were recruited to come to North America, many said later, the advantages of emigration to the Selkirk colony had been exaggerated. It had even been suggested to some of them that the Red River country might be a good place to grow citrus fruit.

Sailing from Europe through Hudson Bay, there is no record of their individual disenchantment with emigration, but in all likelihood they began to discount the possibilities of citrus farming when their ship got stopped for nearly a month in the summer ice flows on the way through Hudson Strait. For the most part, things didn't get better for the Swiss after they arrived at Red River. Almost none of them knew how to farm, or hunt. They wouldn't have come naturally to trapping or fur trading. More importantly, they knew they had been lied to. They had been tricked into coming to North America, and they were resentful because of it. Not surprisingly, the bulk of the Swiss packed up and left on the Red River Trail within a few years of arriving.

The largest group of immigrants at Fort Snelling, including many of the remaining Swiss settlers, came after a winter of heavy snows in 1826, when a sudden spring thaw flooded the Red River Valley. More than 200 of the Swiss settlers left the Forks for the United States as soon as the valley dried enough to allow them to get away, and another 100 Scottish, French Canadian and Métis settlers soon joined them on the trail. It's possible that one or two of Pierre Bottineau's half sisters, from his father's first marriage to an Assiniboine woman named Techomehgood, were among them.

In the months that followed, and for two generations after that, settlers from the north regularly made the move down the Red River Trail to the milder climate and freedom of commerce found on the upper Mississippi. The Indian agent at Fort Snelling, Major Lawrence Taliaferro, wrote in 1835 that the Red River immigrants living near the fort already totaled nearly 500 people, and he wondered, probably rhetorically, if there were any settlers left in Selkirk's old colony.

Taliaferro posed a reasonable question. The entire Red River population at the north end of the trail at that time was about 3000 people. Still, settlers at the Forks had increased their numbers to a point where it had become a firmly established community, with a population large enough to spin off members for the new settlement near the fort at the south end of the trail.

Chapter Six

The Soldiers and the Count

I n 1823, United States Army Major Stephen H. Long returned to the upper Mississippi just six years after his first expedition into the region. That visit had sparked a recommendation to build Fort Snelling. He also attempted to find the source of the Mississippi River. Long came north for a second time to explore the Red River Trail and mark the international boundary where it crossed into British territory at Pembina. As a result of that work, details of the trail were documented for the first time.

Long's party left Fort Snelling (then still called Fort Saint Anthony) on July 9. His force included 21 soldiers, an astronomer, a geologist, a zoologist and a black slave. Joseph Renville, a half-Sioux partner in the new Columbia Fur Company, who operated a trading post near Lake Traverse, served as a guide during the first half of the journey.

Along with the official members of his expedition, Major Long allowed an eccentric Italian count named Giacomo Constantino Beltrami to come with the party. The count, who had first met Long at Fort Snelling only a few days earlier, managed to talk his way into the expedition's ranks as a guest. He had been hanging around Fort Snelling since the spring, looking for adventure and hoping to see a battle between the Ojibwa and the Dakota, so he could write about the fight for publication in Europe. By the time Long arrived, Beltrami was already beginning to complain about the uncooperative Aboriginals whose nonviolence was messing up his literary plans.

Whatever else can be said about the Italian nobleman, he did not lack courage, although, at times, common sense seemed less evident. Just a few days before he departed with Long on the trail north, Beltrami went buffalo hunting. According to his Métis guide, the count rode directly at several bison and tried to kill one of the bulls with his hunting knife. Beltrami's attack managed to severely wound the animal, but the count fell from his horse in the process. Once on the ground, he would have surely perished had it not been for a crack shot from his guide's musket, dropping the buffalo dead before it could trample and gore the foolish Italian.

Once Long's expedition got underway, the men followed the Minnesota River from its mouth at Fort Snelling to the river's headwaters, where it crossed the short stretch of marsh that constituted the Continental Divide, and then continued almost due north along the east side of the Red River. Long followed the Red to where its waters emptied into Lake Winnipeg, deep in British territory. From the lake, he turned the expedition southeast on the Winnipeg River, passing through Lake of the Woods and the Great Lakes to Ohio and the settled parts of the United States.

What we know of the Red River Trail in 1823 comes mostly from journals written by William Keating, the geologist on Long's expedition. During the course of the journey, Keating noted several Red River carts on the trail, as well as some of the early immigrants escaping south to the new settlement on the Mississippi. He also told of a group of Métis returning with their carts from a summer buffalo hunt, and he recounted details of meetings between members of the expedition and several bands of Native people.

Long's expedition left Fort Snelling with its members divided. Part of the group oared and poled up the Minnesota in boats, others went overland, following the river through the valley, but both parties camped together each night. After six days, advancing only 130 miles to a spot near the present city of Mankato, Long decided the progress on the water was too slow, and he knew that, in all probability, it would get slower as the expedition moved farther up river. He sent nine soldiers home to Fort Snelling, and after that the expedition became a strictly cross-country adventure on the Red River Trail.

One reason Long sent soldiers back to the fort was to save rations, but he also decided the nine men were no longer required. Long had been warned before he left that he might meet a band from the Sisseton branch of the Dakota in the valley who were in a bellicose mood. The Sisseton, however, appeared to have left the region to hunt buffalo farther west. As a result, Long felt less need to include and feed so many soldiers.

Beltrami, on the other hand, stayed with the expedition, although by this time Long had probably already begun to doubt the wisdom of his decision to bring him along. Almost from the beginning, the count complained about the way the American Army was treating a gentleman of his standing, which paved the way for the count's eventual departure.

Long had wanted the two halves of his forces to stay as close together as possible, so those on land had to make their way in the river valley instead of on the higher ground above, where the going would usually have been easier. In the valley, forests "of maple, white walnut, hickory, oak, elm, ash and linden, interspersed with grape vine," along with other vegetation, made travel more difficult than on the plains above. The route close to the river was also, at times, so marshy that the men "could not proceed without much danger to themselves and their horses." In one or two instances, the ground was so soft they were obliged to construct causeways made from logs, or even outright bridges, to get through it with the animals.

Despite these initial problems through the valley on horseback, once voyaging on the water was abandoned, Long proceeded overland from the great bend in the river with new vigor. He had 21 horses (nine were ridden by officers and gentlemen, including Beltrami; 10 were packhorses; and two were lame and couldn't be used at all for several days). Meanwhile, the rank and file of soldiers walked. Because Long was now able to stray farther from the water, the plains above the valley floor allowed the expedition to proceed on a more direct route at a much faster pace.

On the first day after leaving the river, Keating reported that the men went across some "fine rolling prairies" on a path that took them along the north side of the valley. On July 18, he noted that "the monotony of a prairie country always impresses the traveler with a melancholy, which the sight of water, woods, etc. cannot fail to remove." Keating said the river valley had been out of sight all that day. On the prairie, there were few springs and a scarcity of firewood for cooking, which made the journey more difficult. He added that the temperature reached 94°F in the shade, when shade could be found.

In addition to the heat and monotony of the prairie, the greatest annoyance of all turned out to be mosquitoes, which Keating said, "arose in swarms as to prove a more serious evil than can be imagined by those who have not experienced it." The expedition would find no more torment from mosquitoes anywhere on their journey than they did while in the vicinity of the Minnesota River.

"The mosquitoes generally rose all of a sudden about the setting of the sun," Keating wrote. "Their appearance was so instantaneous that we had no time to prepare ourselves against them. Whenever we had the good fortune to encamp previous to their sallying from their hiding places, our great object was to complete our evening meal before they commenced their attack... and we have not unfrequently [sic] been so much annoyed by these insects as to be obliged to relinquish an unfinished supper."

The expedition passed several Sioux villages where the residents were away hunting buffalo. Later, after they arrived at the headwaters of the Minnesota and then on the headwaters of the Red River, the group came across Dakota people who greeted them in a friendly manner. Long's dealings with the Sioux on the trail lay in sharp contrast to the experiences of several others on the Red River Trail about the same time. Before leaving Fort Snelling, Long learned of people who had been killed on the route a year earlier. The expedition passed near present-day Grand Forks, on the east side of the Red

River, opposite from where, only a few weeks before, a Scottish blacksmith and most of his family had been set upon and killed by a band of Sioux. The only survivors in that incident had been two children whom the Natives carried off, keeping them for several months.

Long's expedition, however, met with little of the troubles with the Dakota that others had encountered on the trail. On Big Stone Lake, in today's South Dakota, the Sioux invited the men to a series of meals, one immediately following another. The final entrée, dog meat, was a particular favorite for the Dakota, and the members of the expedition had to appear appreciative no matter if their appetites had already been sated or if their tastes tended toward delicacies other than those offered. Dog meat, said a journalist writing of a later Sioux feast, tasted worse than mule meat, but somewhat better than wildcat.

After Long left Big Stone Lake, the expedition continued north on the trail for a short distance and spent the next few days at Joseph Renville's Columbia Fur Company post at Lake Traverse, where the men were treated to similar hospitality by the nearby Sioux.

A couple of days after leaving Lake Traverse, Long's men came as close to open violence with Natives as any encounter they had over the entire course of the journey. A few miles downstream from where the Bois de Sioux River joins the Otter Tail, near today's Breckinridge, Minnesota, about 40 Natives met up with Long's forces. The Natives were part of the Wahkpakota, the "Leaf" band of the Dakota, who apparently often lived in the forested areas of eastern Minnesota.

Not long after the first group of Natives arrived, others from the same band joined them.

The Natives outnumbered Long's men several times over and behaved in what Keating described as "an insulting manner." All carried guns or bows, and some carried both weapons. Keating reported that Long wanted to immediately order an all-night march to separate his men from the Natives, but it was impossible because a few members of the expedition were away hunting. Long could not leave anyone behind, so he made camp near the river, with the menacing Natives close at hand.

Sometime after midnight, with the Natives apparently asleep nearby and all of his men having returned from hunting, Long ordered everyone onto the trail, and his expedition escaped. The next morning, the Wahkpakota apparently decided against following, and a fight was avoided.

It was also along the upper Red River that Keating noted that the plains had become "apparently boundless." Rocks, Keating said, were rare, but the land was often pebbly, as if it were once the bed of some river or lake, which of course would later be shown to be true. What we call the Red River Valley isn't really a river valley at all; it's the exposed bottom of the now vanished Lake Agassiz.

Keating wrote that the expedition, once it started north from Lake Traverse, saw "an abundance of game." In addition to the herds of buffalo and elk, the Red River Valley was home to grizzly bears, wolves and all manner of waterfowl. The naturalist Earnest Thompson Seaton recounted seeing a large wolf on the west side of the river at the edge of Winnipeg as late as 1880.

On his first visit to the West, around the same time, Theodore Roosevelt had hunted in the Red River Valley and recorded shooting in excess of 400 grouse, geese, snipes, sharp-tailed plovers, ducks and grebes—although the shooting, he said, had not turned out to be as good as he expected.

In the days following the expedition's encounter with the Wahkpakota, Keating described the plains:

> *The calm repose of these prairies seemed to be more disturbed during the night, as the lowing of the buffalo on the west bank of Red River were then frequent and distinct.... The beautiful and boundless expanse of the prairies, as seen by the bright moonlight which we enjoyed during this period, the freshness of the night air, the stillness of the scenery, interrupted only by the melancholy howlings of the wolf, and the prolonged lowing of the buffalo, the recollection of the dangers which had lately threatened us... all these were likely to suggest to the mind melancholy yet not unpleasant reflections.*

It's thought that the people using the Red River Trail during the early years usually followed the more dependable branch of the trail in the higher country west of the Red River, but the usefulness of the trail's competing branches can be clearly demonstrated by Long's decision to march north relatively close to the river on its east side, something that would not happen during wet years when the same areas were almost impossible to cross. The early 1820s had been comparatively dry, however, and as a result, following a route relatively close to the east side of the Red was apparently common. Long's expedition passed others going south on the same route.

At Lake Traverse, Long added a Hudson's Bay Company trader to the expedition who took on the role of guide to replace Joseph Renville. Métis cart drivers also joined here, and they apparently had no qualms about starting up the east side of the Red because they had experience on the trails. Only after the group reached Pembina would Long's expedition cross to the west side of the river, and that had nothing to do with the quality of the trail. It was to pay a visit to the strategically placed village on the border between American and British territory in the Northwest.

At the time of Long's visit, there were about 60 log cabins with an estimated 350 somewhat transient residents in Pembina. Most were Métis, but a scattering of Swiss and Scottish settlers who had come to rely on the Métis' buffalo hunts lived there as well. Only the Scots were good settlers, wrote Keating—by which he probably meant that only the Scots were what he thought of as good farmers—who would therefore, he supposed, advance western civilization in so remote an area.

The day the expedition arrived at Pembina, the community was nearly deserted. Most of the residents had been away for a month and a half on the summer buffalo hunt. In all probability, the young Pierre Bottineau and his family were among them.

The few people still in Pembina when Long arrived were short of food, as was the expedition itself. Fortunately, the hunters and their families returned the day after Long reached the settlement. "The procession," Keating wrote, "consisted of one hundred and fifteen carts, each loaded with about 800 pounds of the finest buffalo meat." The hunting party included about 300 people, with women and children among them, perhaps including as many as 11 members of the Bottineau family.

Long's primary assignment at Pembina was to determine the location of the 49th parallel. The settlement at that time lay almost directly on the international line, about a mile north of the town's present location, but when observations were taken to determine the boundary, Long found that only one of the cabins actually lay north of the border. He placed an oak post at the line with the initials "G.B." (Great Britain) carved on one side and "U.S." on the other. Later, when a joint United States and Canadian commission determined the official border in 1872, Long's more primitive calculations for the boundary location were found to be a few yards too far south.

Long's instructions from Washington had been to follow the 49th parallel east to Lake of the Woods before continuing back to the United States along the international boundary. At Pembina, however, he learned that such an undertaking, because of the region's swamps and marshes along the Roseau River, would be impractical. Instead, he ordered his men to continue north across the international boundary to the settlement at Red River. At the head of the trail he sold the expedition's horses and outfitted his men with canoes. The group then paddled the river to Lake Winnipeg. From there, they canoed the old fur-trade route to Lake of the Woods, and then, essentially, followed the border to Rainy

Lake and the Great Lakes, where the expedition found its way back to settled parts of the United States.

While at Pembina, Beltrami had to sleep in one of the community's log cabins, along with other members of the expedition. For the Italian count, the cabin was a flea-infested hovel, and he demanded that Long have a tent set up for him instead. Long refused, and Beltrami, rather than continuing with the army, headed into the Minnesota wilderness on his own to search for the source of the Mississippi River. Actually, he wasn't quite alone when he left. He took a Métis and two Ojibwa hunters along as guides.

U.S. Army lieutenant Zebulon Pike had incorrectly named Cass Lake as the source of the Mississippi River 20 years earlier, but even at that time, in 1805, fur traders in the area, and certainly Natives, could have taken him to the stream at the foot of a lake that the ethnologist and geographer Henry Schoolcraft later named Itasca. In all probability, Beltrami's original guides knew the approximate area where the headwaters of the great river could be found when they left Pembina. Still, Beltrami was off in search of a river whose source, he wrote, "was absolutely unknown" to the world.

Not surprisingly, the count eventually "discovered" what he said was the source of the Mississippi. Beltrami's original guides abandoned him, put off by the Italian's strange behavior, so he was on his own for several days. One big problem Beltrami discovered was balancing himself in his birch-bark canoe. He found the process so troublesome that, instead of paddling, he resorted to dragging his canoe along northern streams with a rope.

Eventually, Beltrami came across two Ojibwa men who agreed to help him find the source of the river. And with new guides, the count found a lake he claimed held the headwaters for both the Mississippi and Red rivers. The Red River, the count said, was fed by "seepage" from the lake he named Gulia, after a lady friend in Italy. He said the Mississippi began as a small stream at the outlet of the same lake. Beltrami, of course, was wrong on both counts. Later, a Minnesota county and state forest, among other things, were named after the Italian count who had spent a summer roaming frontier Minnesota before returning to Europe to write about his adventure.

Chapter Seven

The Fur Companies

When Long's expedition passed through Red River in 1823, its members saw a community that, after 10 years as an official settlement, had just begun to put down roots. The newly found success was largely the result of the growing Métis population, the tenacity of Thomas Douglas' Scottish settlers and the tendency of former fur-trade employees to move to the settlement at the end of their contracted service. Sometimes, the Hudson's Bay Company encouraged these former employees to move to Red River. This allowed the company to rid most of its territory of its former employees and their Métis families, even if the moves created an enlarged community of former employees at the forks of the Red and Assiniboine rivers.

Despite the slowly increasing number of settlers, the Selkirk Colony would never have grown much larger than an isolated fur-trade outpost if it had not been for the rising prominence of the Red River Trail, the trail that Stephen H. Long followed north to get to Red River. In the early years, the trail was necessary to Selkirk's settlement because it brought the community additional commerce and sometimes vital supplies, but especially because it ameliorated the almost complete isolation in which the people otherwise found themselves.

Red River's link to England, with a single ship arriving and departing each year through Hudson Bay, magnified the settlement's isolation rather than reducing it. On the other hand, Fort Snelling—Red River's link to civilization at the southern end of the trail—was closer to the settlement than the northern outpost on the bay, where the journey to England began. In addition, the trip south could be made whenever the traveler decided to go. Fort Snelling might have been an American outpost, but for the people of Red River, it offered a portal to the world outside, at least for those who were willing to follow the Red River Trail.

From the first days of the trail, in the 1820s, the American community at Fort Snelling, on the eastern edge of the Western wilderness, had a comparatively easy river link to St. Louis, as well as to the river towns in Illinois as people and consumer goods steadily spread westward. It was a long road to civilization for Red River's people, but the trail provided the community with its easiest connection to the rest of humanity. The Hudson's Bay Company's sailing ships across the North Atlantic would never be enough. The long fur-trade canoe route to Montreal was almost out of the question. Red River and its trail to the Mississippi had to develop together, one dependent on the other, for the settlement to survive and maybe thrive.

During the western fur trade in the last quarter of the 1700s, goods were transported east and west, from Montreal through the Great Lakes, to both the upper Mississippi and Red rivers, eventually all the way to the Missouri and Saskatchewan country and even beyond. After a while, the HBC started bringing goods deep into the continent's western interior much more economically through Hudson Bay. Once the Red River Trail started being used, there was a new option, one that turned out to be more practical yet.

After Long's border survey in 1823, dozens of Pembina Métis, and a few Scottish settlers, moved north of the line, either to the settlement at The Forks or to White Horse Plains, just upstream on the Assiniboine River. Here, the Hudson's Bay Company promised the Métis free land so long as they lived in British territory. While the migration north bolstered the population at Red River, the exodus from Pembina wasn't strictly patriotic. The HBC, aided by the Catholic Church, encouraged the Métis to move north because the company wanted to get them as far as possible from the temptations of trade with the Columbia and American fur companies on the Red River Trail. The company was also worried that that skirmishes frequently fought between Métis and Sioux on the hunting grounds near Pembina would spill over to the north side of the border.

George Simpson, the HBC's governor, made a deal with Cuthbert Grant, who had been the Métis leader at the Battle of Seven Oaks in 1816, to settle at White Horse Plains. At the same time, Simpson encouraged several other prominent Métis from Pembina to move north as well, including Pierre Bottineau's father, Charles, along with his family. As a man who could wield influence among the Métis, Charles Bottineau was singled out and encouraged, like Grant, to make the move north, in the hope that others at Pembina would follow his lead. As further inducement to the Métis, the

George Simpson ran the Hudson's Bay Company in North America from the early 1820s to 1860. After the international boundary was surveyed in 1823, he encouraged the Métis living south of the line to move north.

Catholic Church at St. Boniface closed its mission in Pembina and set up shop instead at White Horse Plains.

As the 1820s began, although Red River looked much as it had during its initial years, its old divisions had begun to fade. The community began to grow and take on a feeling of permanence. The North West Company continued to press the Métis to drive the Selkirk settlers away, but both groups, it seemed, had become part of the community. And with the majority of people at Red River clearly Métis, the economic threat some of them originally feared from Selkirk's settlers seemed farfetched. The Métis already there were growing steadily in numbers, and more former fur-trade employees from all over the northwest were moving in with their Métis families every year. Several dozen Scottish farm families were no menace.

Then in 1821, a monumental change took place in the fur trade. The Hudson's Bay Company absorbed the North West Company in an amalgamation that turned the huge northern fur trade into a monopoly for the English company. In some ways, the takeover seemed inevitable. The intense competition between the two organizations could not be sustained indefinitely, and the conflict of 1816 at Seven Oaks, with the legal battles that followed, seemed to sour the Métis on the fight. At the same time, the constant struggle to keep up with the HBC began to sap the competitive strength from the smaller North West Company. The North Westers never stopped trying to stir up resentment against the settlers and the Hudson's Bay Company, almost right up to the time of the amalgamation, but the Montreal firm had essentially lost heart in the battle. The long fight with the much larger English fur company seemed hopeless.

The Hudson's Bay Company had several things going for it in its battle with the Canadian company. For one thing, the HBC had deeper pockets and could withstand more competition than its smaller rival. The most important advantage, however, was the cheaper cost of bringing in English trade goods through Hudson Bay, rather than through Montreal and the long water route the North West Company used to cross the continent through the Great Lakes. The smaller company's employees had always been more aggressive traders, but in the end, transportation costs made its business model unsustainable. The North West Company just couldn't compete.

After the amalgamation, all over the great northern fur country, from Lake Superior to the Pacific, in places where there had been two fur posts, one from each company, the Hudson's Bay Company would now need only one. Sometimes not even one would be needed, and posts from both companies would close as the HBC, without real competition anywhere in the territory, consolidated and streamlined the fur trade. Longtime fur company employees from both firms suddenly found themselves out of work.

Bottineau's father would have been one of them if he hadn't already moved to the independent life of the buffalo hunt. Virtually all of the voyageurs who had paddled canoes from the fur country to the Great Lakes and back again every summer lost their job. Many of these former employees moved back to the Red River country and turned to the independent and nominally illegal fur trade at the first opportunity.

Most were just part-time traders, mixing the exchange of furs in with hunting, trapping and subsistence farming in the Métis way to make a living. Others continued in the fur trade on a grander scale. One of the traders who lost his job in the amalgamation, Kenneth McKenzie, teamed up with William Laidlaw, the manager of the Hudson's Bay Company's experimental farm at Red River, to start the Columbia Fur

Company in 1821, almost immediately after the amalgamation was announced.

McKenzie and Laidlaw were joined in this undertaking by three independent traders tied to the upper Mississippi trade: Robert Dickson, James Kipp and Joseph Renville, the guide for Long's expedition in 1823. Only Renville could claim American citizenship, because he had been born to a Sioux mother south of the new international line, but even he had fought on the British side (the country of his father) during the War of 1812. In addition, Renville had spent much of his life working for both the North West and Hudson's Bay companies. Still, the Columbia Fur Company started business on the American side of the 49th parallel, with its most important post, at Lake Traverse, near the halfway point on the Red River Trail.

In the fur trade, there had never been any consistent recognition of national sovereignty, except where patriotic notions might be a business benefit for one competitor over another. Traders, in both the United States and Canada, were overwhelmingly of British or Canadian (either French or English) origins. Enlisting the help of affiliated fur traders in St. Louis, partly to cement their role as an American company, the Columbia partners moved into the upper Mississippi and Missouri River trade. They competed with John Jacob Astor's American Fur Company between the Red and Mississippi rivers and with the St. Louis firm of Bernard Pratte and Company in the upper Missouri River country. Significantly, and deliberately, the new company also competed for furs with the Hudson's Bay Company's operations to the north wherever it could entice the trade away from the senior company.

The Columbia's post on Lake Traverse on the Red River Trail served as a supply point for posts that eventually stretched as far west as the Yellowstone, Teton and upper Missouri rivers. It was the Columbia, it was said, that first used Red River carts on the trail between Lake Traverse and fur posts downstream on the Minnesota. With several smaller posts in the Minnesota Valley, including one at the river's mouth near Fort Snelling, the Columbia was largely responsible for the first well-marked cart trail along the Minnesota River Valley.

Traditionally, fur traders traveled downstream by water from Big Stone Lake, just across the low Continental Divide that separated Big Stone from Lake Traverse. Because river levels were undependable on the upper Minnesota, the Columbia traders started shipping furs overland by Red River carts, all the way downstream to Traverse des Sioux, near today's St. Peter, Minnesota. The river was more dependable from that point, and continuation on the overland trail through the forests of southern Minnesota was more difficult. Still, a cart trail from Traverse des Sioux to the Mississippi was used regularly, too, as the Columbia and others brought more trade goods up and down the developing trail.

Although much of the Columbia Fur Company's business came from the area immediately around its western posts in American territory, a significant amount of furs was siphoned south from western Canada that would otherwise have gone to the Hudson's Bay Company. The Columbia's founders knew the richest fur country was in the north. Indeed, their business plan took advantage of the company's proximity to Canadian furs from the beginning. Despite the

Columbia's location in the United States, the company competed in the Red River and the Blackfoot country, where Kenneth McKenzie had years of experience, to draw furs whenever it could from the north side of the international boundary. The company's interest in the trade at Red River, itself, stemmed from the existing trail that already carried settlers and independent traders into its territory.

After the American Fur Company absorbed the Columbia in 1827 and took over its trade in the Red River Valley, it opened a string of new posts near the Canadian frontier, from Grand Portage near Lake Superior to Pembina and the Turtle Mountains, on today's boundary between Manitoba

A series of sheds near Fort Garry served as Andrew McDermot's store at Red River.

and North Dakota. The plan was to increase trade coming from the north, once again at the expense of the HBC. Just as importantly, Columbia founder Kenneth McKenzie, who stayed on to work for the American Fur Company, moved farther up the Missouri and began competing directly with the HBC for the Blackfoot trade in places where HBC traders had always feared to go.

The HBC, of course, was aware of the dangers of competition from below the border. And the company knew that hunters, trappers and traders from the north side of the boundary going, literally, over to the other side would fuel the competition. In 1823, after Long's expedition came up the Red River Trail to mark the border at Pembina, the HBC closed its post there, which for more than 20 years had been its most important fur fort in the area.

Instead of the trading post at Pembina, where it would have to compete head to head with the Americans, in 1824 the HBC built a new post, a larger stockade it called Fort Garry, at Red River, 60 miles to the north. It also opened a small, seasonal trading post at a cabin just north of the border near Pembina after it had enticed as many of the Pembina Métis as it could to move farther north, beyond (it hoped) the temptation to smuggle furs down the Red River Trail to the United States.

To counterbalance the effect of the American Fur Company's new posts near the international boundary, the HBC selected a few independent traders and promised them higher prices for furs they gathered near and below the 49th parallel, furs that would otherwise be traded to the Americans. The HBC also allowed some of these most-favored independent traders to import trade goods of their own from England, on the ship that brought annual supplies from Britain to York Factory, the company's port on Hudson Bay.

Of all the independent traders who went to work for the Hudson's Bay Company in this way, Andrew McDermot became the richest and most important. McDermot, who often worked closely with a Métis trader named James Sinclair, had immigrated to North America from Ireland in 1813 to work for the HBC, but he became so discouraged at his lack of advancement that he quit in 1824 and went into business for himself.

The HBC held a monopoly in the fur trade, but its stores at Fort Garry were geared to a specialized business. The company wasn't yet interested in the sale or trade of domestic goods in the local economy, so McDermot became what was known at the time as a petty trader, providing goods to the settlers that the larger company was, for some time to come, unable, or unwilling, to furnish.

While the Hudson's Bay Company concentrated its business on the fur trade, McDermot turned to the settlers, giving them a place to barter wheat, cattle and other products in which the HBC had little interest except for securing their own provisions. McDermot began ordering domestic trade goods on the company ship that made yearly deliveries to York Factory. Because he had to arrange the transportation needed to get the goods south from the northern port, he soon owned a fleet of York boats for the job, which led him to develop a freighting business that worked on contract, usually to the HBC, throughout the territory. At some point in the mid-1820s,

McDermot also began bringing in a few goods from the south, up the Red River Trail from the Mississippi.

McDermot's store at Red River appeared like nothing we think of today as a frontier retail establishment. It certainly didn't have much in common with the scrupulously tidy HBC store at the fort, where the company displayed goods behind long, varnished counters that separated the customers from the merchandise. McDermot, instead, operated out of a series of sagging sheds built, one after another, in the yard outside his home, in the heart of the growing settlement near the HBC's fort. On the surface, everything seemed cluttered and disorganized. There was no store counter and the goods in each shed seemed to be scattered haphazardly about, illuminated only by an open door or oil lamp.

But the apparent disorganization masked a shrewd and ordered business mind that brought McDermot almost immediate wealth in his new ventures. All through the 1820s, the young Irishman found economic opportunities while mostly working within the great fur company's restraints. From the HBC's point of view, at least in the beginning, McDermot provided them with a service. The company could not handle all the needs of the settlers and buffalo-hunting Métis in the community, but McDermot and other petty traders could do so. After all, even when McDermot bought furs, he sold them to the HBC anyway, so everybody was happy. In addition, some of his furs were bought from other independent traders south of the international line, so what did it matter if a few goods were also smuggled north as a consequence of that trade?

When the HBC began paying traders a premium for furs bought near the international boundary, McDermot was there to take advantage of the higher prices. Only later, when he found it more profitable to thwart company policy, would he turn wholeheartedly to the smuggled fur trade on the Red River Trail. And only then would the HBC turn against him.

As things turned out, paying McDermot and others who worked along the border higher prices only partially mitigated John Jacob Astor's American Fur Company encroachment, but the HBC had other advantages over Astor's traders. For starters, the HBC was far bigger than the American firm. It could withstand more competition and afford to pay

Fort Garry was built in 1823 after the Hudson's Bay Company closed its post in Pembina.

unprofitably higher prices in the region longer than its competitor. And English goods were in more demand from the Natives than American goods.

To augment its independent traders north of the border, the English company soon began encouraging Métis traders to move their businesses south of the line and then bring the furs they collected back north. One of these traders, Augustin Nolin, started a rumor at Pembina that a cholera epidemic had spread to the American Fur Company post there, which, though untrue, dampened that company's trade with the Natives for several months.

But the whole thing was an expensive nuisance for the HBC. The border situation had also become problematic for the American Fur Company by that time. It was an irritant of which both companies wanted to rid themselves. In 1833, the two firms reached an agreement to stop direct competition. The American Fur Company closed most of its border forts in exchange for a yearly payment of 300 British pounds from the Hudson's Bay Company. Meanwhile, the English company was satisfied the sum could be made up, several times over, by cutting prices for furs bought near the border to rates prevalent in the rest of its territory.

But nothing could stem the tide of free trade sentiment developing in Manitoba. When the HBC shut off the higher prices it paid its independent traders, the traders naturally turned to the south to sell furs deeper in American territory, where they could get higher prices. Prominent traders like McDermot protested to the company about the lower prices in the north, while smaller traders like Sulpice Desautel, Pierre

Bottineau's brother-in-law, loaded a few Red River carts with furs and slipped away in the night to sell furs down the trail in the United States. Bottineau may have occasionally gone along with him. Soon, McDermot was doing the same thing, and the cart trains following the Red River Trail grew longer and more numerous.

The Hudson's Bay Company had, inadvertently, stimulated the free trade it railed against by cutting off its independent traders. If they couldn't sell their furs for a high enough price to one company, the traders would find another firm with higher prices down the trail.

The HBC had been unconsciously promoting free traders all along. Its policy of paying higher prices to non-Natives for furs than it did to Natives encouraged both Métis (who were considered non-Native) and white traders to become middlemen. The Métis and white traders bought furs from the Natives at the going rate, which was unlawful according to the company, and then resold the furs to the company at the higher prices reserved for non-Natives.

It was only a small step for these part-time trappers and traders to start moving their furs south of the border to American Fur Company traders where they could get a better price.

Chapter Eight

Smuggling on the Red River Trail

The Red River Trail connected the dots for a route that would eventually bring an avalanche of commerce to Selkirk's colony and become the pathway for virtually everything that was imported or exported from the settlement. By the late 1830s, free traders had shortened the trail, using a new, more direct route to connect Red River with the Mississippi. Instead of following the Minnesota River Valley, the new branch of the trail left the Red River along its upper reaches, usually somewhere on or near the Bois de Sioux, north of Lake Traverse.

The new route angled southeast on a more direct path across Minnesota to the upper Mississippi. This course, through western and central Minnesota, changed from year to year, as one path or another gained or lost favor. But the trail essentially stayed north of streams flowing into the Minnesota, instead roughly following a route that led to the Sauk River and then followed that stream until it arrived on the Mississippi near today's St. Cloud.

The new branch could be troublesome because it passed through lake country, past prairie marshes, creeks and sloughs. Because of the difficulties encountered along the way, the trail's path tended to shift from season to season, and year to year, as the cart drivers tried to avoid the worst mud holes and stream crossings. Often, it seemed, the long Métis cart trains avoided one bad spot in the road by exchanging it for a new one. Still, the route constantly got shorter as time went on and became several days faster than the original trail along the Minnesota. It was also considered safer. The new route essentially crossed a no-man's land on the southern edge of the loosely defined border that separated the territories of the Ojibwa and Sioux, avoiding the Sioux heartland along the original trail in the valley.

In the early 1840s, when leadership in the confederation of traders that made up the American Fur Company changed, the deal with the Hudson's Bay Company fell apart. Once more, American border posts sprang to life, most notably at Pembina, where Norman W. Kittson and Jolly Joe Rolette set up shop. From the beginning, this new post, organized through Pierre Choteau's St. Louis firm, with Henry Hastings Sibley overseeing the federation of traders in Minnesota, took larger and larger cart trains of Canadian furs south every year.

At Pembina, the trade was almost entirely a collection point for furs smuggled across the border, along with buffalo hides from both sides of the international boundary. Kittson seemed to have struck a good business plan, and commerce was so brisk for a few years that his post almost appeared to be the head of the trail.

On the north side of the boundary, Andrew McDermot was still the largest of the independent traders at Red River. Twenty years after going into business—first in a sweetheart deal with the Hudson's Bay Company, and then smuggling furs down the Red River Trail—he was universally known as the richest man at Red River. It was said that only a rare bush failed to get plucked when Andrew McDermot walked past. At Red River, those who needed to borrow money, rent a house or enter into most any form of business arrangement usually went first to McDermot. Kittson, too, had gone to visit Red River's leading businessman before he started his venture at Pembina. Although it's not known what kind of a deal the men made, McDermot certainly entered into some sort of early business arrangement with the Pembina trader.

What had begun as Selkirk's little settlement on the lower reaches of the Red River became, in the 1840s, a different place than it had been when the trail first started a generation earlier. Slowly the economy had become stronger, in large part because of McDermot and the other free traders who depended on the Red River Trail. The free traders were the innovators and risk takers at Red River. It was free traders who brought new goods to the settlement and had the best contacts with the outside world.

The Hudson's Bay Company sent its profits back to Europe, but every year the free traders brought proportionately greater wealth to themselves and the local economy. By the middle of the 1840s, McDermot owned most of the land in what was to become downtown Winnipeg. In fact, for a time, the budding city was known as McDermotville.

Agriculture, though practiced seriously by only a minority of residents at the settlement, had been firmly established since 1830, but it was plagued considerably by the isolation of the Red River Valley. Farmers had nowhere to sell their grain or cattle except in the limited local market or occasionally at Fort Snelling. Cattle, scarce in the colony in the initial years, became so plentiful they lost most of their value. Although there was a small trade in tallow sent to Europe through Hudson Bay, cattle became an export commodity, sent down the Red River Trail to the United States. In 1835, a group of emigrants left Red River for the upper Mississippi driving a herd of cattle equal in size, it was said, to all the cattle that had ever been brought north from the United States in the early days of trail.

Sometime around 1840, the population at Red River grew to more than 4000 people, with the Métis by far the majority. Relatively well-off retired company officers, with Native or Métis wives, brought a touch of affluence and a source of popular leadership to the frontier outpost, and the children in these families added to the ever-expanding population of Métis. A few emigrants continued to flee down the Red River Trail every year, but the settlement at The Forks went on growing.

But in a frontier community where the majority of people depended to one degree or another on the revenue of the fur trade, there was no way an English company could demand allegiance to store and trader when Kittson's new fur post just across the border on the Red River Trail had better prices. For a time, the Hudson's Bay Company at Red River paid only half of the $3.25 Kittson gave for a beaver pelt. It paid five shillings for a buffalo robe that could bring $2.50 smuggled across the international line. By the 1850s, the same skin could get $3.50 south of the border.

Smuggling became a way of life, in one way or another, for more and more people at Red River. Peter Garrioch, the Métis trader who supervised the construction of a new branch of the Red River Trail along the Crow Wing River in 1844, provided a lively account in his diary of smuggling goods down the trail to Kittson at Pembina. Garrioch tells of loading a cart with furs after midnight in Red River at the home of James Sinclair and spending almost three days following a circuitous route over the prairie.

Garrioch avoided the initial leg of the Red River Trail close to the river, where potential smuggling might be expected, and took his cart on a lesser-used road going west across the open plains from Red River. Eventually, he turned south to cross the border west of Pembina, at a place still known as Smugglers Point. In one instance, when he saw another cart approaching, Garrioch hid his furs behind some ragged shrubbery on the prairie. Then, after visiting with the people and agreeing to meet them later at a destination well north of the border, he waited until they were out of sight before reloading his cart and continuing his journey to Kittson's trading post at Pembina.

As the buffalo numbers declined, especially after about 1830, the Métis of Red River took to hunting in larger and ever more disciplined and organized ways. Growing animosity between Métis and Sioux also contributed to a desire for larger hunting parties. The Métis gathered for their biannual buffalo hunts near Pembina and, usually after hunting to the southwest on the Missouri Coteau or near the Turtle Mountains or farther west along the international boundary, came back to trade at Kittson's post. Even if the hunt had occurred north of the border, they returned to Pembina to sell hides. The American trade in buffalo robes was an easier and for many years a more lucrative source of income for the Métis than beaver pelts—mostly because the Americans were closer to eastern markets where the robes were worth more.

It was a trade that seemed to suit the Métis because it was more exciting than the traditional fur trade and was more social. And it was easy enough to stop in Pembina to sell hides and sometimes pemmican to the Americans, a simple business decision. The Métis traded where they could get the best price, and after selling skins in Pembina they usually continued north to offer pemmican to the Hudson's Bay Company at Fort Garry, where that commodity was in more demand.

Meanwhile, the Canadian-born Kittson complained bitterly to American authorities about the Red River Métis, who sold part of the proceeds from the hunt north of the border. It was a practice, Kittson claimed, that cost him thousands of dollars in lost revenue every year, and he petitioned the government to get the American army to demand the Métis stay and live on the south side of the boundary if they intended to hunt American buffalo.

Kittson's demands were somewhat ironic, given his Canadian roots and that so much of his business came from the north side of the border. The Métis hunting patterns, of course, had been established well before there had ever been an international boundary. Besides, many of the Red River Métis, like Pierre Bottineau, did move south, and the Red River Trail remained as important as ever to their livelihood. While most of the buffalo hunters lived for most of the year in and around their homeland at Red River, the Métis went on trading wherever they pleased, and they kept doing it for as long as the buffalo lasted.

As Red River grew, the Métis became more powerful, increasingly seeing themselves as a nation of people on the plains. Ironically, as the nation of the Métis grew in numbers and spirit, the first stirrings of their eventual demise in status also surfaced in the colony.

The union of white and Aboriginal had long been the practice of the fur trade. The family bonds it created strengthened local commerce and community ties. Some white husbands did walk away from their Native or Métis wives and children at the end of their contracts with the fur company, returning to their former homes alone, but others did not. Some brought their families with them back to Europe or Quebec. Others, in lasting relationships, sent their offspring away to school back in Canada or overseas, or to the United States, and then remained in the fur country themselves after retirement from the company.

Generally, the society of the fur trade accepted these informal white and Native marriages, known as *à la façon du pays*. And as the settlement at Red River grew, the Métis became a counterforce to the rule of the Hudson's Bay Company, partly because of their numbers but also because of the important roles they found in local commerce and foreign trade and the quasi-military role they took on as hunters and protectors of the settlement.

But in 1830, when the Métis as a group had already started to become more powerful, the social structure of the community at Red River was disrupted. George Simpson, governor of the Hudson's Bay Company in North America, traveled to Scotland, where he married a white woman, his cousin, Frances Simpson. The marriage itself wouldn't have been particularly noted at Red River, except Simpson already had a reputation for his many sexual liaisons during his decade on the western side of the Atlantic. His reputation was such that when the Anglican missionary William Cochrane told Peguis, the Ojibwa chief on the upper Red River, that to become a Christian, Peguis had to chose only one of his four wives and get rid of the rest, Peguis told the missionary that he would choose just one wife only after Simpson had done the same.

Simpson was said to have fathered a lot of Métis children—with one estimate, probably exaggerated, pegging his offspring as high as 70. Métis trader James Sinclair's sister, Betsy, had been one of Simpson's Native wives, and Simpson sent her off to be married to the chief trader at a fur post on Hudson Bay after she bore him a child. When Simpson left North America to retrieve his new bride, he sent his Métis wife of the time to visit her sister—where she gave birth to a second son—without telling her the purpose of his trip across the ocean.

In his journals and letters, George Simpson showed no more respect for his sexual companions than he did the Aboriginal or Métis people generally, referring to a partnered woman as the "commodity" or his "bit of brown." When he brought Frances to the fur country, they settled at Red River, about 20 miles downstream from Fort Garry, where Simpson built a residence in the new, and somewhat extravagantly constructed, Lower Fort Garry.

In their new home, the Simpsons may have been the king and queen of the fur country, but their social life was dreadful. The couple allowed no Métis women, except servants, inside their door. This included the Métis wives of several prominent, white Hudson's Bay Company officers. And at Red River, if Métis women were ostracized as social inferiors, the only female companionship left of high enough order for socializing with Mrs. Simpson would have been the wives of Protestant clergymen. Simpson spent much of his time away from Red River, inspecting fur posts across the continent. Not surprisingly, Lower Fort Garry turned out to be a lonely and unpleasant place for Mrs. Simpson, and after a few years, the couple arranged for her to live at a new home in Quebec.

But Simpson, who ran the Hudson's Bay Company for 40 years, had lit a fire. He had made it clear to everyone that he and his wife considered the majority of the people at Red River, the Métis, to be of a lower caste. Prejudice had always been present at Red River, but Simpson legitimized it for the company officers, white clergymen and social climbers who lived or moved there in later years.

As time went on, the Métis population at Red River continued to grow. (In 1870, when Manitoba became part of Canada, the Métis made up over 80 percent of the population.) In the same way, the Métis people's sense of uniqueness and nationhood continued to be hailed. But after Simpson's marriage, the divide between the Métis and the Hudson's Bay Company appeared greater than before.

A rift had been exposed in the community, which was hard for the most loyal Hudson's Bay Company employee, if Métis, to ignore. While the company was tolerated in its role as employer and accepted as the de facto government of Rupert's Land, for Métis with the wherewithal to trade somewhere else where they could get higher prices for furs and robes, it was simply one more grievance to hold against the company. They loaded up a cart and slipped across the border to sell goods to the Americans at Pembina or down the Red River Trail in St. Paul. For many, like Pierre Bottineau, it was one more reason to leave Red River and establish a home on the Mississippi at the south end of the trail.

Chapter Nine

On the Trail with Pierre Bottineau

S ometime in the 1820s, several members of Pierre Bottineau's family moved to the upper Mississippi, close to Fort Snelling. Bottineau visited there as early as 1830, when he was about 13 years old. By that time, of course, the young man, like other Métis youth of the plains, was on the cusp of taking his place in the world. He would have been able to catch and tame any of the half-wild horses in the Métis *remudas* pastured on the open prairies near Red River, and he would already have become an accomplished rider. He would have also taken part in the annual buffalo hunts.

For the young Bottineau, fresh from the prairie, Fort Snelling's proximity to the outside world—with St. Louis only a steamboat ride away—must have stood in sharp contrast to the isolated outpost at Red River where the people lived surrounded by a universe of wilderness in all directions. Bottineau's father was a respected hunter who usually participated in the summer and fall hunts. The Natives, in fact, called the elder Bottineau "Mustus," or "Buffalo" Bottineau. (This was a nickname that Bottineau's French-speaking comrades good-naturedly changed to "Mustouche" or "Mustache.") It is said that the senior Bottineau kept nearly a dozen good buffalo horses and was known as something of a horse trader.

Horses, of course, were a mark of wealth among the Métis, which, at that time, made Mustus Bottineau a wealthy man. After the death of Charles Bottineau sometime in the mid-1820s, the family had lived an even more nomadic and precarious life than before, sometimes with his mother's people, sometimes with other family members, including a half-brother and sisters from Charles' first marriage. Pierre Bottineau also appears to have stayed for some time with Antoine LeCompte, who was a well-known guide and an old friend of his father's from his early years with the North West Company.

LeCompte, who trapped, hunted buffalo and worked as a voyageur and messenger for the Hudson's Bay Company, apparently began grooming the young Pierre Bottineau early for the wilderness trail. In addition to hunting and trapping, the pair traveled as far north as Hudson's Bay, as far west as the Missouri River country when the buffalo hunts took them there and as far south as the Mississippi. On at least one early trip south, Bottineau delivered mail for the Hudson's Bay Company to Fort Snelling and then continued another 200 miles south to Prairie du Chien.

According to one report, on a trip to the upper Mississippi sometime in the early 1830s in late November, Bottineau, LeCompte and a third man were following the Red River Trail on the river's east side when they almost met with tragedy crossing the Red Lake River. As the men were attempting to ford the ice-choked river on a raft fashioned from a Red River cart with extra logs tied to its sides for buoyancy, the vessel began to flounder with river ice piling against its side at a fast spot in the current.

LeCompte and the other man were unable to swim, so Bottineau had them each straddle a log and hang on while he poled the swamped cart for the opposite shore. Before he could get there, however, the ice-clogged current swept them around a bend in the river, grounding the improvised raft on a sheet of ice still some distance from land. Bottineau grabbed a rawhide rope, tying one end around his waist and the other to the cart. He started to walk across the ice but fell through almost

Pierre Bottineau in a photo taken about 1855, when he was already a well-known guide.

immediately and had to swim for shore, breaking the thin ice with his arms as he swam. Once on shore, he pulled the cart, along with his companions, safely through the ice.

Sometime around the middle of the 1830s, Bottineau began making regular trips up and down the trail to Fort Snelling, as a guide and trader. When he was 19, he married Genevieve LaRonce at Red River. Four months later, in March 1837, he was on the trail again, escaping the blizzard with Martin McLeod, before paying another visit to Fort Snelling. After that, he seems to have lived, at least seasonally, near the fort, finding occasional work with the American Fur Company's Henry Hasting Sibley or taking cattle, immigrants or goods up and down the trail.

Bottineau could have continued working with the Hudson's Bay Company, at the north end of the trail, but the American Fur Company paid more. And there was also the matter of prejudice. The HBC discriminated against the Métis, or half-breeds, as they were generally known by others at the time. French Canadians also suffered from some of the same limits to advancement at the HBC, so why not go to work for Sibley instead.

One story from that time took place when Sibley asked the young guide to deliver an injunction against a competitor, a trader named Sylvanus Lowry. Sibley said that Lowry could be found, with about $30,000 worth of cash and trade goods that belonged to him, at a trading post 150 miles northwest of St. Paul. Sibley also told Bottineau that three others were already on the trail to warn the man to escape, so speed was necessary. Bottineau grabbed a horse and a short time later caught up to one of the men riding to warn Lowry. For several miles the two men raced along the trail together, each spurring his horse to get ahead of the other.

When they were finally forced to stop for the night, it was at a camp on the trail where one of Bottineau's brothers happened to be staying, which allowed Pierre to get a fresh horse. Unfortunately, the two other riders out to warn Lowry were also at the camp. One of these men, who had already had some sleep, slipped away early in the night. When Bottineau discovered his absence, he had to leave, too, and to catch up, he galloped into the dark, "in danger," he said later, "of breaking my neck and killing my horse." All through the night he rode, until the sun came up the next morning.

Soon after daylight, Bottineau saw his competitor ahead of him on the trail. Instead of racing to get ahead, he slowed down, staying out of sight. Then, finally near the trading post where Lowry was to be found, he spurred his horse on, passing his rival and arriving in time to present the man with Sibley's petition.

In 1838, Bottineau led a party of 40 families moving south from Red River to the Mississippi. He also brought along 20 head of cattle, several bundles of furs and other merchandise of his own to sell when he got there. The journey was apparently uneventful, except for having to repeatedly deal with hostile Sioux along the way. Bottineau negotiated for safe passage several times during his journey, paying for the privilege of travel on the trail each time with gifts of tobacco and flour.

By that time, frontier settlements were well established at both ends of the Red River Trail, and in a clear reflection of

Bottineau's conflicting interests, he had official residences in both Red River and on the Mississippi. An 1840 census at Red River noted that Bottineau owned six oxen, six cows, four calves, one plow and four carts in the community. The same year, he was listed as living on the Upper Mississippi in several American historical accounts. An attractive aspect about the Red River Trail, for someone like Bottineau, seemed to be that no matter what end of the trail he found himself, something, or somebody, needed to be taken to the other end. In a similar way, Bottineau continued to take part in the annual buffalo hunt on the Dakota prairie west of Pembina, as he increasingly shifted his base of operations to the upper Mississippi.

In the summer of 1840, Bottineau helped guide a large ox-cart train that left Red River at the beginning of June, in what turned out to include a tragic affair on the trail. Just one day after leaving Red River, Bottineau's old mentor, Antoine LeCompte, or Le Gros, as he was sometimes known, joined the party. LeCompte came with another guide named John Bird and their charge, Thomas Simpson, a Scottish cousin of Hudson's Bay Company's governor, George Simpson.

Thomas Simpson had spent several years in North America working for the Hudson's Bay Company, part of it in an administrative job at Red River and part of it exploring the northwest Arctic coast. He had come to work for the HBC at the invitation of his prominent cousin, but once he arrived at Red River, he soon lost favor with his powerful relative. George Simpson, in fact, grew to loath his new employee, hating him so much that he sent him to the Arctic for a couple of years.

But in 1840, Thomas Simpson had completed his work in the north and was back in Red River on his way home to Scotland. Conflicting reports suggest he may have demonstrated erratic behavior before leaving the settlement, but once on the Red River Trail, Simpson seemed constantly agitated. A couple of days after joining Bottineau's cart train, Simpson told the guides he wanted to push ahead of the main group, so LeCompte and Bird, along with LeCompte's son and another Métis guide named James Bruce, all traveling horseback, led Simpson south on the trail, leaving Bottineau behind with his train of Red River carts.

Three days later, Simpson complained of illness and wanted to go back to the main party, and his guides agreed to take him. After spending most of a day on the trail north, the five men stopped to camp on the Turtle River. As they were getting ready to set up a tent, Simpson, appearing increasingly upset, suddenly shot and killed LeCompte and Bird at close range. Simpson explained to Bruce that he had killed the two men because they were planning to kill him, and he offered Bruce 500 British pounds to take him back to Red River.

Instead, Bruce and LeCompte's son escaped on their horses, riding back to the main party, where they enlisted help from Bottineau and several others. Riding hard, the group returned to Simpson's camp. Stopping a short distance away, they called out Simpson's name. Nothing was heard for a moment, but then a single shot cracked in the silence. The men took cover, some firing their guns in the direction where the shot had been heard. Two of the men crawled through the grass toward the wagon. They found Simpson dead, apparently from his own hand, lying on the ground near the bodies of Bird and Bottineau's old mentor, Antoine LeCompte.

The men buried the three bodies on the prairie where they found them and then continued their journey. At the time, the stretch of the Red River Trail the group had been on was considered part of Iowa Territory, which stretched north from Missouri to the Canadian border. Distant authorities in the south were willing to accept the version of events as reported by the participants when they reached Fort Snelling.

Since then, several historians, including Simpson's brother, Alexander, have questioned the story of the deaths on the trail. Alexander Simpson offered a theory that his brother had actually been murdered and had killed Bird and LeCompte in self-defense, before dying himself. A later theory suggested it was none other than George Simpson behind the murder. No official investigations of the deaths were ever made.

Chapter Ten

Crow Wing

Four years after Thomas Simpson's death, Peter Garrioch, one of the Métis free traders operating out of the Red River Settlement, cut a new branch of the Red River Trail along the north side of the Crow Wing River, through Ojibwa territory, to create a route that was several miles shorter than what had become the trail's usual path farther south along the Sauk River. The new trail had the added benefit of avoiding the northern edge of Sioux territory.

People were always developing short, new branches for the trail, cutting off a wet section here or altering the path to include a new river crossing there, or making an easier route through a wooded area in some other place, but the changes were often of little consequence as they just substituted one poor section of trail for another. Garrioch's new road, however, was a significant undertaking. Starting at the mouth of the Crow Wing, it cut through some of the hardest to penetrate forest and swamp land in Minnesota until it emerged on the open prairie on the east side of the Red River Valley near today's Detroit Lakes. From there, the trail followed the beach ridges that rolled north all the way to the Manitoba frontier.

There had always been a route on the east side of the Red River, at least in dry years, but before Garrioch, travelers kept to an essentially straight north/south line through northwestern Minnesota, relatively close to the Red, and rejoining the better-used trail at about its half way point, west of today's Fergus Falls. Garrioch's new branch, on the other hand, was well north of the other trail and stayed in the trees in Ojibwa territory because Sioux war parties had been particularly menacing through much of southern Minnesota and eastern Dakota in 1844.

At the time, the Sioux were ill-disposed toward the Métis because they competed for the already diminishing buffalo herds but also because the Métis were often related to, and traded with, the Ojibwa, a traditional enemy of the Sioux. Several generations earlier, when the Sioux inhabited the forest country of northern Minnesota and some of what became Ojibwa lands to the east, things had been different, but when the Ojibwa obtained guns from European traders ahead of the Sioux, they drove the Sioux away. In the open country to the west, the Sioux learned the benefits of horses ahead of the Ojibwa and could be driven no farther.

There's a rock at the edge of the prairie near my home that the Ojibwa consider sacred. To this day, there are Ojibwa people who occasionally stop at the rock to leave tobacco and other offerings. According to the story, a wounded Ojibwa hunter who was being pursued by a band of mounted Sioux once hid behind this rock while the Sioux galloped past. The rock is somewhat small for a man to hide behind, but it took pity on the hunter and, magically, helped conceal him from his enemies.

The Métis used Garrioch's Woods Trail, which passed just east of this rock, whenever they thought it prudent to stay clear of the open plains and keep close to the trees in Ojibwa territory. Here, they would be less likely to attract the attention of the Sioux. Making their way west from the Mississippi to the edge of the plains on the Woods Trail allowed the Métis cart trains to stay in the safer Ojibwa forested areas on the trip through the middle of Minnesota. When the trail turned to the north, it stayed on the east side of the Red River, still on the edge of Ojibwa territory, where it could skirt either side of the tree line along the sand and gravel ridges, all the way to Red River.

At the mouth of the Crow Wing River, where it flows into the Mississippi, a village grew up after the trail came into use there, and for a few years in the mid-1800s, the town of Crow Wing came to prominence because of its strategic location near the southern end of the Red River Trail.

In many ways, Crow Wing resembled the border community of Pembina at the other end of the trail. Both started as Métis villages, Crow Wing near the southern terminus of the trail, Pembina near the northern. For some, these communities seemed like the unofficial starting or stopping points for the trail, places where the real wilderness either began or ended, depending on the direction of travel. That's why the "Woods" branch of the Red River Trail was sometimes called the Crow Wing Trail in the north, while people in the south sometimes called it the Pembina Trail.

Crow Wing probably began as a seasonal settlement for the Ojibwa after they expanded their territory in northern Minnesota in the 1700s. One of the earliest accounts of activity in the Crow Wing area, according to Warren's *History of the Ojibway People*, tells of a battle between the Sioux and Ojibwa in the 1760s. Several groups of Sioux, after suffering losses in northern Minnesota and Wisconsin, met at the Falls of St. Anthony to plan raids on the Ojibwa, who by then occupied most of the traditional Dakota land in the north.

The Sioux paddled up the Mississippi, turned into the Crow Wing River where they stopped to camp and then made a loop through Gull, Leech, Cass and several other northern Minnesota lakes. From the north, they started down the Mississippi again to make their way home. Before they had gone far, the Sioux warriors came upon a pair of Ojibwa hunters. But the Ojibwa saw the Sioux first, and they fled down the river to warn the people of Sandy Lake that their enemies were on the way. Many of the men of the community were away at the time, so despite the advanced notice, the Sioux killed many of the Sandy Lake people and kidnapped several young women before the others escaped.

What the Sioux warriors didn't know when they finally moved on, ecstatic with victory, was that they were heading into a trap. Downstream on the Mississippi, the Ojibwa who had been away from Sandy Lake and knew nothing of the Sioux raid on their village, came across tracks the Sioux had made when they had stopped to camp at the mouth of the Crow Wing River. The Ojibwa knew the Sioux were bound to return on one river or the other, so they devised an ambush a short distance south of the mouth of the Crow Wing. It was at a place where the Mississippi narrowed below banks as much as 50 feet above the water. The Ojibwa dug trenches on these banks and hid. Scouts watching for the approaching Sioux sent word that the enemy was on its way.

The Sioux stopped briefly at the mouth of the Crow Wing before resuming their journey. At the bend in the river where the Ojibwa lay in ambush, Sioux camaraderie and the force of the current brought their canoes closer together, making it easier for the Ojibwa to kill them. Some of the Sioux were still singing a victory song when the Ojibwa let go with arrows and bullets.

As soon as the shooting started, several of the captive women flung themselves into the water, purposely overturning Sioux canoes in their escape. As the chaos increased, scores of Sioux were killed, though many made it downriver and a few swam to the opposite shore, where they retreated south.

Unwisely, the surviving Sioux regrouped and attacked the fortified Ojibwa position above the river. Despite their larger numbers, the Sioux were easily driven back. The next morning, they attacked again. This time, after more losses, they retreated downriver to their homes. With this defeat, and fearing additional Ojibwa retaliation, the few Sioux who remained in northern Minnesota, in what had become Ojibwa territory, escaped to join others in the Minnesota River country to the south.

The Sioux have a legend of the fight at the mouth of the Crow Wing River, only their story tells of the wife of one of the warriors. She dreamed her husband would be killed if he went north to fight the Ojibwa and so she pleaded with him to stay home. The husband ignored her request. Instead, he asked the spirits to ensure his eventual return, and he promised his wife that she would see him again.

About the time when the Sioux warriors were due home, the young wife went to the river to brush her hair, using the water to reflect her image like a mirror. As she sat on the bank, a body suddenly swept past her reflection in the current. The woman instinctively reached out and grabbed one of its arms. When she pulled the body to shore, she saw it was her husband. His promise to return had been fulfilled.

Traders began moving into the Crow Wing area on a seasonal basis only a few years after the great battle between the Sioux and Ojibwa. A visit from one of these early traders, in the late 1700s, led to the name for the band of Ojibwa known as Pillagers. The Pillagers were one of the earliest Ojibwa groups to settle in Minnesota and, as such, they developed a reputation for their prowess in war against the Sioux. Their name, however, came about for a different reason than any fighting and pillaging they may have done.

In 1781, part of this Ojibwa band was camped about 10 miles upstream from the mouth of the Crow Wing River, near Pillager Creek and today's town of Pillager, when a trader arrived carrying goods he'd brought from Mackinaw Island. By the time he reached the Crow Wing, however, the trader had become ill. The Ojibwa had a large number of pelts to barter, but he refused to start trading until he felt better. The Natives put up with the delay for a time, milling about the merchandise that had been put out to dry, until one of the men took a piece of cloth, explaining that he would pay for it in furs once the trader was ready to bargain.

This apparently spontaneous act led immediately to another of a similar nature and then another. As the situation deteriorated for the trader, his store of whiskey was discovered. At this point, people began drinking as well as pillaging from the trade goods on hand. The sick trader and his men, fearing for their lives, left their merchandise and fled downstream where the trader reportedly died from his illness.

The following spring, feeling somewhat remorseful for their actions and also hoping to entice another trader to the region, a delegation of Pillager leaders canoed to Mackinaw Island, in the Straits of Mackinaw, between Lake Michigan and Lake Huron, to present traders with several packs of beaver pelts as a demonstration of good faith. According to legend, the British commander was aware of the pillaging incident that now gave the band its name, but he accepted their gesture of friendship. In return, he offered the Pillagers presents, including a bale of goods he said should be taken back to the community for distribution among the people.

Not long after these goods were passed around, however, a smallpox epidemic spread through the community. Band members maintained that their people had been intentionally infected with the disease, but no proof exists. Still, the following June, Jean Baptiste Cardotte reported that "all the Indians from Fond du Lac, Rainy Lake, Sandy Lake and surrounding places are dead from smallpox."

In the first years of the 19th century, while Pillagers remained in the area, permanent trading posts began to appear at Crow Wing. Allan Morrison built a post in 1823 on land that, more than 20 years later, would become part of the Crow Wing town site. A few years after that, he operated a post on Crow Wing Island, just across the Mississippi. For the next few years, Morrison and other traders worked in the area. Then, in the fall of 1844, everything changed when Peter Garrioch built his new branch of the Red River Trail

Garrioch's line of carts carried supplies for the new fur post that Norman W. Kittson, along with Henry Sibley, James Sinclair and Joseph Rolette Jr., had organized at Pembina. Kittson, who had come to the Wisconsin and upper Mississippi country a decade earlier, had been recruited by Sibley to handle furs in the Red River Valley, along with a few posts along the Minnesota and on the James and Sheyenne rivers in North Dakota. From Garrioch's diary we know of the difficulties encountered cutting what became the middle leg of the Woods Trail from the Mississippi River to existing trails on the plains east of the Red River. Tensions had been growing between the Sioux and Ojibwa, and by extension the Métis, through the 1830s and early 1840s. Several serious skirmishes had occurred in 1843.

Then, in the summer of 1844, after a group of Métis near Devil's Lake west of the Red River mistook a band of Sioux hunters for Pawnee, open warfare nearly broke out. The Métis killed one of the Sioux, believing they had come across Pawnees hunting outside their territory. Quickly realizing their mistake, the Métis tried to make amends for the error, but the damage had been done. The Sioux effectively shut off trade on the trail for everyone for the rest of the year, and intermittent skirmishes and battles took place along the route for nearly two decades afterward.

That autumn almost nobody got through Sioux Territory. Garrioch knew he couldn't get Kittson's trade goods over the old Minnesota River route, and he was worried about the Sauk River branch of the trail as well, so he hired Pierre Bottineau to guide his train of carts through central Minnesota. As they prepared for the journey and more information came in, however, Garrioch decided that plan was too risky. After more delays, he finally decided to take his carts farther north along the east side of the Mississippi, all the way to the mouth of the Crow Wing River.

Here, well within safer Ojibwa territory, where even the Pillagers would offer no deterrent to travel comparable to the warring Sioux, he found a way around the trouble. Once again, Garrioch tried to hire Bottineau to guide his carts through the woods and swamps along the north side of the Crow Wing River, but Bottineau was busy with freighting contracts, seeing that Mississippi keel boat crews went north from St. Anthony. Attempts to find other guides also proved fruitless, so at the end of September, Garrioch and his crew struck out by themselves through the thickly forested wilderness along the Crow Wing River.

The season was growing late and Garrioch needed to get started with his trail if he hoped to arrive in Pembina before winter. But from the first day, cutting the new route through the trees and wetlands met with unforeseen troubles and unexpected physical difficulties. Soon after leaving the Crow Wing Island trading post, two of his men—first one, then another who was sent to find the first—got lost. On the second morning, a group of Ojibwa from Red Lake stole four horses The horses were recovered after a chase, but the day after that, two more horses were taken. This time Garrioch had to go all the way back to the trading post to retrieve the missing animals.

The most daunting problems, however, came with the work of cutting the trail through the thick swamps and forests in the middle of Minnesota, an area that early French traders had noted as almost impenetrable. They called it *bois forts* ("tough trees"). Garrioch recorded in his journal that on some days the new road inched forward only a single mile. On an average day, on the early part of the trail, his men could cut only three and a half miles of road.

The traders took just over two weeks to make a rudimentary path on the north side of the Crow Wing River, as far as a ford just below the mouth of the Leaf River. No mention is made in Garrioch's journal about the place being a traditional crossing place, but it might have been. More than 40 years earlier, John Baptiste Cadotte had wintered near the spot with a number of traders, one of whom owned or employed a black man. A tale is told that sometime over that winter, the trader and the black man began to get on each other's nerves. A fight started, and when it looked as if the black man might get the better of it, the trader's Ojibwa wife stabbed and killed him.

Garrioch's party also came across a black man on the trail eight days after crossing the ford to the south side of the Leaf River. The meeting took place when the trail breakers reached Otter Tail Lake. By this time, the group was completely out of provisions, but the black man, perhaps the well-known Minnesota trader George Bonga, had plenty of supplies. He was in the area trading for furs with a band of Pillagers. Garrioch noted that despite the Natives' fierce reputation, they showed little of their reputed bellicose nature. According to his journal, the Pillagers "evinced no such disposition as we expected they would be inclined to do, from every representation that we had ever heard of their character as a tribe."

Garrioch traded with Bonga to get dried fish and wild rice for his crew. For himself, he traded a fur cap for 40 fresh fish and a cod line he could use for tethering horses. Horses, Garrioch said, were the one thing the Pillagers bothered with during the two days the trail cutters spent recuperating at Otter Tail Lake. Although Garrioch repeatedly explained to the Natives that his horses were in poor shape and needed rest if they were to make it to Pembina, the Pillagers paid no attention. They kept riding off on the animals when Garrioch wasn't watching. Then, after an hour or two, they would sneak back, pretending they had never been away.

For more than a week after leaving Otter Tail Lake, Garrioch continued cutting trails through the low hills and forests of northwestern Minnesota known as the Leaf Mountains, until he finally broke through the trees near today's Detroit Lakes. "The vast and beautiful prairies we had longed for burst suddenly upon our view this evening," he wrote in his journal. "We could not but hail the prospect with accents of the greatest satisfaction and liveliest gratitude."

The men had made it out of the woods, but they still spent the better part of a month crossing the Red River Valley to Pembina, often trudging through deep snow. In following years, the trail to Crow Wing, on the east side of the Red, cut a more or less direct route along the succeeding ridge lines south from Fort Garry and Pembina to Detroit Lakes, and then angled markedly southeast to Crow Wing, but Garrioch and his men floundered over the frozen prairies in what he described as "a circuitous manner."

Garrioch's cart train finally crossed the Red Lake River somewhere below the site of today's city of Crookston, then crossed to the west side of the Red River north of today's Grand Forks, North Dakota, near the mouth of the Turtle River, before finding its way to Pembina. It was already early December, late in the trading season, but Garrioch had created a new branch of the Red River Trail, with only some details of river-crossings and favorable beach ridges to follow on the east side of the river left to be worked out.

Garrioch's new route was shorter and often faster than taking the trail on the west side of the river, though it was also often boggy in the *bois fort* of northern Minnesota and was usually considered more difficult than the branch of the Red River Trail that ran along the Saulk River farther south. Garrioch had cut the trail during an unusually dry fall and was able to build it through places that would have typically been bogs and marshes in wetter years. This made things easier for Garrioch, but subsequently, of course, the trail to Crow Wing reverted to more typical conditions. Often in spring, and sometimes in summer, it was the wettest, most difficult route to the upper Mississippi.

To get around the troublesome stretch, cart trains on the east side of the Red often used a connecting link a few miles west of Detroit Lakes that led to the Sauk River Trail. This linking trail left the Crow Wing route on a mostly direct route south to the other major branch of the trail, where the cart trains could then continue through the lake country and open prairies to the Sauk River Valley. The primary advantage for the trail to Crow Wing was avoiding Sioux territory, and cart trains took advantage of it for that reason starting the summer after it opened.

From then on, the Woods route became the alternative branch of the trail. In winter, when ice and snow covered the

James McKay, known as the strongest and toughest man at Red River, prided himself on taking George Simpson from Crow Wing to Fort Garry in just 10 days, partly by arranging for spare horses along the trail.

wet areas and made travel by dog sled easy, most everyone took the short route to Crow Wing. In the 1850s, Joe Rolette and Norman Kittson would cover the distance between Pembina and St. Paul by dog team in less than 20 days. When the Hudson's Bay Company started using the Red River Trail, its governor, George Simpson, regularly made the trip between Crow Wing and Fort Garry with horses in just 10 days.

A Métis employee named James McKay oversaw these trips, and he took pride in getting the Hudson's Bay Company's governor to Fort Garry exactly at noon on the tenth day of the journey. McKay was a big man, by all accounts weighing over 250 pounds, with exceedingly broad shoulders and a bull-like chest, although without exceptional height. His strength was legendary. According to a story, one day while he was working in his garden at Red River a stranger rode up. The man jumped from his horse and announced that a Red River resident had told him McKay was the toughest man in the territory. The stranger had come, he said, to knock that reputation down a peg or two. Without saying a word, McKay belted the man in the chops, then picked him up like a sack of turnips and threw him over the fence.

"Did you want anything else?" McKay called after him. "No," the man groaned from the ground. "If you'll just throw me my horse, I'll be on my way."

Another story often told about McKay's strength was that he was sometimes able to pull Red River carts out of mud holes at river crossings on the trail, even if they had become so bogged in the mire that horses were unable to do the job. In one such incident, in the summer of 1850, he was with James

Sinclair and two of Sinclair's teenage daughters when a horse got bogged down at the crossing of the Red Lake River. Sinclair's daughters were on their way home from boarding school in Illinois at the time, and the faltering horse left them and their cart stranded in the middle of the river. McKay walked into the stream, unhitched the horse, put himself between the shafts and hauled the young girls to solid ground on the other side of the river.

James Carnegie, the Earl of Southesk, went along with George Simpson on the trip between Crow Wing and Winnipeg in 1859, when a particularly wet spring seemed to keep McKay in the mud and water for much of the journey. Instead of taking the usual 10 days, it took a day shy of two weeks for McKay to get his charges to Fort Garry because of the wet conditions.

According to Carnegie's memoir of the adventure, the group of under a dozen men left Crow Wing on May 20, but didn't get to Red River until June 1. Early on the first day, after goods, horses and men had been ferried across the Mississippi, the going was pleasant enough, through pine forests "where the ground was tolerably sound and hard, though intersected by a few trifling swamps." At noon, having been on the trail since daybreak, the group finally stopped for a breakfast of eggs, bacon and biscuits, and then a quick return to the trail, where "the swampy places grew more numerous." In some spots, the wagons had to be unloaded, and McKay and his fellow Métis *engages* had to carry the baggage and supplies through the swamps on their shoulders so that heavy carts and horses wouldn't get bogged down in the mud.

The going was somewhat better the following day, but the day after that, a less-than-friendly band of Pillagers tried, unsuccessfully, to stop McKay, who was riding at the head of the procession. There was a short tussle with one of the Natives before McKay threw him aside and the group rode off. At first, the Natives tried to stop them again but soon abandoned the cause, shooting over the heads of the escaping men as a last farewell.

Later that day, Carnegie said, he threw away a match after lighting a cigar and a leftover ember started a wildfire. The group was following the trail west, however, and the flames spread east with the wind, so with no apparent concern from the man who started it, the fire was left to burn as it pleased. "I never heard to what extent it spread," Carnegie wrote in casual prose of the fire's ravages, "but for hours afterward we could see its lurid glow illuminating the darkness of the distant horizon."

The next day, the group "passed through a wood of fine maples, ironwood and brush not unlike an English forest in appearance." Carnegie also wrote, "Later in the day coming to the top on an ascent, a most glorious landscape opened full upon our view. Far as the eye could reach, swept one enormous plain…."

Once it reached the plain, however, after another day of rain and mist hampered progress again, the group was stopped briefly at the flooded Wild Rice River. Here, McKay had to build a scow from the wheels of an oxcart, lashing two of them together and then stretching an oilcloth across their bowed underside. Additional buoyancy was obtained by lashing four poles to the sides, so that belongings could be ferried across the swollen stream. At that point, the horses were driven across, and the expedition got underway once again.

From there, it was a "weary ride" over a plain so soft from the heavy rains that "the horses went fetlock deep at every step," sometimes sinking to the hocks. "Every brook was a river. Every swamp was a lake," Carnegie wrote. The trail itself, he said, was a swamp.

In the days to come, the weather, briefly, got better and the trail drier, although camped on the south side of the swollen Red Lake River a few days later, Carnegie said, he "could not but wish that everything were safe across." For the next two days the group pushed forward through swamp and prairie, where "grass, nothing but grass," met the horizon all around. They crossed the Snake, Tamarack and both branches of the Two Rivers. At one point, Carnegie stopped for an hour of target practice, shooting dozens of passenger pigeons from the flocks then still plentiful on the plains.

At Pembina, where the group stayed for the night at a Hudson's Bay Company post placed strategically on the north side of the border, Carnegie reckoned the community was "a small and straggling place, not worthy to be called a village." The following day, once again with rain, the men continued through still more swampy country. After one more night on the trail, they stopped for breakfast at a settler's cabin, and later the same morning, they crossed the Assiniboine River and rode at full gallop to Fort Garry, "amidst the firing of cannon and the cheers of a welcoming crowd." More than a century later, Carnegie's family had Southeby's sell a number of Ojibwa and Métis-made artifacts he had collected on his journey.

In addition to being a trading center on the Red River Trail, Crow Wing began to develop into a regional center for the growing lumber industry in Minnesota. In this matter, too, Pierre Bottineau had lent an early hand, freighting supplies north with keel boats and leading lumbermen to appropriate areas for timber cutting to take place. On one expedition, during an encounter with a handful of Ojibwa near Crow Wing, one of the Natives threatened to shoot an ox, and Bottineau took after the man with a hot poker. The rest of the Natives also moved on.

By the 1860s, Crow Wing could boast of at least 30 buildings, including three churches, twice that many saloons and over 500 people. In the 1870s, however, the Northern Pacific Railroad crossed the Mississippi a few miles north at Brainard, and the town of Crow Wing slipped into decline. In the late 1870s, Crow Wing had almost disappeared, and less than 100 years later, it became an official Minnesota historical site.

Chapter Eleven

Pembina

Pembina was a meager settlement in December 1844 when Peter Garrioch arrived in town after cutting his new branch of the Red River Trail from Crow Wing. A few of the derelict cabins built and abandoned by the Selkirk settlers more than 25 years earlier were still in use, scattered among the more recent log buildings, bark-covered shelters and teepees that lined the shore along the Red River north of the mouth of the Pembina.

Today, crowded against the Minnesota and Manitoba borders in the northeast corner of North Dakota, Pembina seems to be just another small prairie town. But for a short time in the 1800s, it was the little brother of the budding settlements of Winnipeg and St. Paul. At that time, a visit to Pembina, just below the 49th parallel, was often seen as a welcome diversion from the Red River Trail. On the Crow Wing route, the trail going south from Red River divided after crossing the Roseau River. One branch of the trail continued toward Crow Wing while the other made a loop west into Pembina. After a stop there, another trail out of town made a bend across both branches of the Two Rivers, west of today's Lake Bronson, Minnesota, to rejoin the main trail to St. Paul.

The first people of European descent probably arrived in Pembina before George Washington was president. In 1823, when the American Army's Major Stephen H. Long reached the village, he talked to an old man, a Métis with the last name of Nolin, who claimed to have first come to the area nearly 50 years earlier, or about 1776. Evidence of both North West and Hudson's Bay Company forts here can be documented as early as 1797 in the journals of Charles Chaboillez, a trader with the North West Company. Another trader, Peter Grant, probably set up shop in the area for a season or two a few years before that. Other traders came earlier, although there's no documentation to provide dates or lengths of stay. When Chaboillez arrived at Pembina, his journal notes that a Hudson's Bay post had already been built there. He also refers to earlier fur-trade activity in the area.

Pierre Bottineau's father, who came to the Northwest from Quebec in 1797, first lived at Pembina while working for the North West Company around 1800. The entry in Henry's journal from 1803 reported Charles traveling with his family to the Hair Hills (or Pembina Mountains) with others on a buffalo hunting expedition. In his journal, Henry lamented the use of horses by employees like Bottineau, claiming access to horses encouraged indolence and insolence, as well as making it easier for the men to "burden themselves" with families. Bottineau left that day with a cart and two horses, taking one and a half packs on board the cart along with numerous bags, kettles and other items, including a tomahawk, while Techomehgood, Charles' first wife, followed on foot, scolding and tossing a "squalling infant" about on her back.

In a later journal entry, Henry noted the passing of a young Bottineau son, one of at least six children born to the

Bottineau family before Techomehgood's death sometime around 1812. While the Bottineaus were one of the first families to move away from Pembina, in the 1820s, the transitory nature of life on the plains continued to make Pembina an important place in Pierre Bottineau's life. Both before and after his father's death, and no matter on what side of the border the family lived, they regularly used the settlement as a meeting place before the fall and summer buffalo hunts. And in the 1840s and '50s, other members of Pierre's family, including a brother and a son, moved back to the community.

When the international boundary was finally settled at the 49th parallel in 1818, nobody knew for sure if Pembina, strung out for a mile or so along the Red River, sat on the north or south side of the new border or right in the middle, but the Hudson's Bay Company and Stephen H. Long, in 1823, both with primitive surveying equipment, determined that it was almost entirely in the United States.

Fifty years later, a boundary commission made up of members from both countries put Pembina officially on the American side, though the new line was drawn far enough north that the new Canadian Customs station that had just been built based on the 1823 survey turned out to be on American soil. A local drinking establishment known as White's Saloon ended up half on one side of the border and half on the other. The saloon solved the problem, so the story goes, by painting a white line through the middle of the building. Operating as a Canadian establishment on one side of the line and an American one on the other, business went on as usual without official sanction from either government.

As the 1880s unfolded, the American town site stabilized with the coming of the railroad near the Pembina River, where the town sits today. The older community closer to the border on the American side became known as Huron City and gradually faded away. The town that grew up on the Canadian side of the border, initially called Pembina, too, eventually shifted mostly to the east side of the Red River to become the town of Emerson when the railroad arrived. As the fur trade declined, both the American and Canadian communities went through the booms of the homesteading frontier before fading into the quiet small towns they have become today.

Pembina's extended frontier heritage is probably no better illustrated than with the story of the poker game that determined ownership of much of the present town site, probably sometime in the early 1870s. Jud LaMoure, part owner of a stage line, and later a United States deputy marshal, held the winning hand. LaMoure was a member of the territorial legislature, as was the other card player, Enos Stutsman, who first owned and then lost the property.

The poker game took place in the Levee Hotel in Yankton, Dakota Territory, where the territorial legislature met at the time. The players had been at the table for more than 40 hours when the wager in question took place. Just before the Pembina land was offered into the game, only two players remained. LaMoure, who had four twos, raised the bet by $100, and Stutsman called, with a full house. Although he held what would normally be a winning hand, Stutsman lost his last $100 and a pot worth $3800.

According to the tale, Stutsman then offered to bet a large portion of what became the Pembina town site against the money he had just lost. LaMoure accepted the wager. The cards were dealt, face up, by E.A. Williams of Bismarck. According to the agreement, each man took five cards and was allowed to discard whatever cards he chose in exchange for new ones to replace the discard. The highest hand took the pot, with no additional bets allowed. At the end of the draw, LaMoure won Pembina with a lowly pair of twos.

The original Pembina settlement had been well located to follow buffalo trails west into the Turtle Mountains, northwest along the Manitoba escarpment or southwest to the plains beyond the Sheyenne River. As late as 1830, buffalo were common around the community itself, making the locale a good place for Métis, Native or Selkirk settlers to spend the winter close to a source of food.

It is from Alexander Henry's journals from 1807 that we learn of what may have been the first baby of completely European ancestry born on the northern plains. Some versions of the tale state that the mother was a Scottish lass who found herself pregnant after her young lover left for a job with the Hudson's Bay Company in North America. To find her lover, the girl disguised herself as a boy and got a job with the company to go overseas, too. Other stories say that the pair signed up together, her disguised as a man, and both traveled to North America in the employ of the company so they wouldn't have to be separated.

The real story is somewhat different. The woman's name was Isabel Gunn (at least that's what she called herself when she returned to Scotland from North America), and she really did disguise herself as a boy to get a job with the fur company. She wasn't pregnant at the time, however, and as far as anyone knows, she wasn't chasing after a boy, although it is possible that she left Scotland with one. More likely, she was simply poor, needed a job and was uncommonly resourceful.

In North America, Gunn apparently performed her work satisfactorily, her secret safe from the company, though not from everyone else because she turned up pregnant at the door of Alexander Henry, the chief North West Company trader at Pembina. Although Gunn worked for the Hudson's Bay Company, still posing as a man and using the name John Fubbister, she told Henry that she was unwell and asked him if she could warm herself by his fire. Once inside, she opened her jacket to show the North West Company trader that she was a woman, one about to give birth.

Gunn delivered a baby boy a short time later, but little is known about her life before or after that day. She apparently stayed in North America with her newborn son, James, long enough to fulfill her three-year contract with the Hudson's Bay Company. It's not known if the father of her child was a lover working for the company or another employee who discovered her secret and forced himself on her. The account from Henry's journal seems to support the latter conclusion, but either way, hers was probably the first child born without at least one Native parent in the northern fur country, although mother and son did not stay.

Two other possibilities have been mentioned as the milestone of being the first birth of a non-Native baby, and these births, too, took place at Pembina. The first was the birth of a boy fathered by Pierre Bonga at Pembina in 1802. Bonga, the son of African slaves from Mackinac Island, was Alexander Henry's servant. Later, Bonga became a fur trader, as did several of his sons and grandsons. But Bonga's wife was probably Ojibwa or Métis, not of African descent, so the claim of a non-Native birth would have been in error.

The other claim is that of Madame Marie Anne Lagimodiere's first child, who was born in Pembina in January 1808. Madame Lagimodiere, originally from Quebec, was the first woman of completely European descent to move to the northwest to stay, and it has been suggested that her baby was born before the Gunn baby, but in fact the Gunn baby was born in December 1807.

Within a few years more, however, several non-Native children were born to Selkirk settlers staying in Pembina. In the early years of the Selkirk settlement, beginning the first winter in 1812 and lasting into the 1820s, Thomas Douglas' homesteaders were as likely to live at Pembina as they were to live farther north at their homesteads at Red River. Many spent the warm months at Red River, but then moved to Pembina to take advantage of the hospitality of the *gens libre* and have easier access to the sale or hunting of buffalo there during the winter.

When the border question was determined in 1823, the colonists returned to their permanent homes on the British side of the boundary or moved farther south to Fort Snelling. It was also at this time that the Hudson's Bay Company, along with the Catholic Church at St. Boniface, encouraged the

Métis to leave Pembina and move north. While some went to homesteads in the Red River Settlement and at White Horse Plains farther up the Assiniboine, there were also a few who stayed in Pembina. Others, resentful of Hudson's Bay Company interference with American trade, left for a short time but moved back to the community over the course of the next 25 years.

In the early years of the Red River settlement, Pembina had been the site of the biggest Hudson's Bay Company post in the valley, but after Long's border survey, the company built Fort Garry, in 1824, at Red River. Locating its regional headquarters farther north was designed to shift the focus of commerce away from American traders like Michael Dousman and Joseph Rolette Sr., who were already using the Red River Trail to trade with their northern neighbors.

Dousman, Rolette and other traders in the region south of the border were considered American traders because they operated out of United States territory, but most of them had been born British or Canadian. And most sided with the British during the War of 1812. Their true loyalties, however, were to the commerce of the fur trade, and any company they worked with, no matter what side of the border they lived on.

In the early 1840s, Jolly Joe Rolette, the elder Rolette's son, arrived in Pembina, followed, in 1843, by Norman Kittson. Because of its location near the border, Pembina was poised to take over much of the Red River trade as the community at Red River grew and the power of the Hudson's Bay Company to enforce any part of its monopoly waned.

Kittson was sent north from St. Paul after control of the affiliation of traders that worked in the area under the American Fur Company banner shifted to Pierre Chouteau in St. Louis, with Henry Sibley on the upper Mississippi running the show throughout the region. Kittson, along with Rolette, worked with prominent traders at the Red River settlement, particularly James Sinclair, to assemble furs and other goods smuggled from across the British line. Once the smuggled goods were in Pembina, cart brigades were assembled early every summer to take the furs south to St. Paul.

Especially in the 1840s, while the Hudson's Bay Company still attempted to enforce its monopoly in the fur trade, Pembina could almost be said to be the head of the Red River Trail. Furs came from north of the border, but it was a clandestine trade. Pelts were brought to Pembina on foot, horseback and in Red River carts, but no matter how many pelts were snuck across the international line, or what the method of transportation happened to be, almost all the furs that came out of British territory into the United States were smuggled in some form or another. Carts were loaded at the Red River settlement in the middle of the night. Traders chose routes between the Forks and Pembina on the basis of evasion rather than convenience. Many took a trail west from the settlement before cutting south to the Red River Trail, where they crossed the border about 20 miles from Pembina.

Every spring, Kittson and Rolette assembled ox-cart brigades in Pembina that took the furs to St. Paul. While traffic on the trail did not grow every year through the 1840s, the trend was unmistakable. Even in 1846 and 1847, when the Hudson's

Bay Company convinced Britain to send troops to the area to protect the border (supposedly from American incursions after the Oregon boundary dispute), the Red River Trail was busier than ever. With British troops at Fort Garry, more food was needed for people at Red River, as well as other goods, such as clothing and rum. British currency paid the tab instead of Canadian furs, but traders and cart drivers on the Red River Trail made more money than before, even if British troops did try to enforce the trade laws for the fur company. Legitimate business was so good that, it was said, Andrew McDermot, already rich, never went back to the illegal trade.

After 1849, however, the Hudson's Bay Company virtually gave up trying to enforce the prohibition against trading with Americans. The Red River Trail had done what no competing fur company had been able to do, bring the 200-year-old Hudson's Bay Company to its knees. Once that happened, once the great fur company stopped trying to enforce its monopoly in the fur trade, Pembina lost its competitive advantage. More and more, the ox-carts loaded with furs came down the trail directly from Winnipeg instead of being assembled at Pembina. Still, in 1851, according to Charles Cavileer, the first customs agent and postmaster at Pembina, for hundreds of miles upstream from Pembina, south of the settlement, there were "no houses, no cattle, no sheep," everything was "all wild as nature made it." Pembina was an American border town at the top of a vast wilderness.

A few years later, the Hudson's Bay Company disturbed the idyll somewhat when it built a freight collection point 200 miles south of Pembina at the head of navigation on the Red River, at what became known as Georgetown. But the land in between there and Pembina was still wild. In the winter of 1859, the company's manager at Georgetown, Robert Mackenzie, froze to death on the Red River Trail while trying to reach Pembina.

Mackenzie and a small party of men originally started from Georgetown bound for Fort Garry just before Christmas. The winter had been mild until that point, and the men left with a small caravan of carts pulled by mules. Once on the trail, however, the weather brought deep snow and intense cold. Halfway to Red River, the mules gave out. On December 30, with still more than 100 miles to Red River, Mackenzie decided to look for help in Pembina, another 50 miles from where the party was camped on the Tamarack River.

He departed early that morning, alone and lightly clad in order to make a brisk pace, taking a fist full of pemmican for what he thought would be a day on the trail. His body was found on New Year's Day next to a small tree where he had hung some of his clothes. Evidently he had become delirious, afer searching in the intense cold for the trail to Pembina. According to a story in Red River's newspaper, the *Nor' Wester,* it was apparent from the tracks nearby that Mackenzie had followed the trail for a considerable distance, but then, probably confused and freezing, he strayed from his course between the north and south branches of the Two Rivers.

Instead of stopping to build a fire and camp when darkness arrived, he appears to have spent the night running in circles to keep warm. In the morning, he started again, in the wrong direction for anyone bound for Pembina.

As for the Red River Trail, in the 1850s, when the Hudson's Bay Company finally took to using it, commerce continued to grow. By the end of the 1860s, the number of carts reaching St. Paul every year was in the thousands instead of the hundreds. In the 1870s, steamboat traffic on the Red River began to disturb commerce on the old ox-cart routes, but river transportation was never dependable on the Red, and the trails continued to be used extensively almost right up until the railroads took over at the end of 1879.

Steam locomotives, when they came to the valley, brought a change in the route even before they covered the entire distance between St. Paul and Winnipeg. As the railroad edged closer to Red River, trade goods began to be shipped along the trails to the terminus of the railroad rather than the traditional end of the trail at St. Paul. Pembina's fortunes by this time were already somewhat separate from the fur trade, which had started to decline everywhere.

In some ways, Pembina's heyday continued into the 1850s, when Kittson and Rolette, along with another trader and territorial legislator, Antoine Gingras, made spectacular 18-day dog-sled trips between Pembina and St. Paul. At the time, Minnesota Territory extended to the Missouri River, taking in today's eastern North Dakota, and someone in St. Paul noted that it was difficult to tell whether the Pembina representative was the heavily whiskered Jolly Joe Rolette or one of his sled dogs.

Rolette was known in the legislature for his good humor and practical jokes. His most famous prank as a legislator came in 1857, the year before Minnesota became a state.

Jolly Joe Rolette was known for his good humor and practical jokes. He was born in Prairie du Chien, Wisconsin, but he spent most of his life at Pembina and Red River.

Almost single-handedly, it was Rolette who kept the territorial capital in St. Paul when the legislature voted to move it to St. Peter, a new town near the old Red River Trail stop at Traverse de Sioux. The governor was ready to sign the law to move the capital, but legislative procedures called for Rolette, the chairman of the House committee on enrolled bills, to have the text of the new law certified by committee vote. Once that formality was completed, the bill was to be sent to the governor for his signature.

As it turned out, the job was easier said than done. Rolette wanted the capital to stay in St. Paul, so when he got the official version of the bill, instead of taking it to his committee for approval, as stipulated by the rules, he absconded with it to a secret location in a nearby hotel. For the better part of a week he hid out, drinking and playing poker with a few friends, until it was too late to get the bill signed before that session of the legislature ended. The governor signed a copy of the bill that was drawn up without Rolette's official sanction, but a local court disallowed it. The governor, the court said, needed to sign the actual bill. As a result, the capital of Minnesota stayed where it was, in St. Paul, and Rolette left for Pembina a few days later on the Red River Trail.

Rolette made much of his Métis roots, although his blood ties to the Aboriginal community were actually obscure. He was born in Prairie du Chien, Wisconsin, a Métis community, but his father, who traded for the American Fur Company in the region, was French Canadian. His mother was also from Quebec, although she had a Quebec grandmother with some Aboriginal ancestry. As a boy, Rolette attended boarding school in New York. But in Pembina, and on his trips to St. Paul, he dressed and acted the part of a Métis hunter from the plains. Perhaps he too closely identified himself with the Pembina Métis, for at the height of his notoriety, Pembina was already in decline.

In the 1850s, largely because of the Red River's tendency to flood, much of the commercial activity in the area on the south side of the border shifted to St. Joseph, at today's Walhalla, when Norman Kittson transferred most of his local operations there. By this time, many of the great cart trains originated north of the border (Kittson opened a trading venture there as well). Soon, Hudson's Bay Company goods started coming down the trail along with many of the company's free-trading competitors, who started shipping goods all the way to St. Paul.

But the fur trade was changing. The boom years were over. While traders like Kittson changed with the times, investing in steamboat companies, railroads and the growing cities of Winnipeg and St. Paul, Rolette stayed with the Pembina Métis. For a short time, he moved to Winnipeg to live with his in-laws. A little later, when he took a job as a United States customs officer at Pembina, he was nearly broke.

By the end of the 1850s, the little community on the border was once again undergoing a change in character. For years it had played a supporting role in the commerce of the region, and for a time a prominent role. When Joe Rolette and Norman Kittson ran a trading post at Pembina, buying goods smuggled from north of the border, cart trains by the dozens and then by the hundreds bound for St. Paul with their buffalo skins and furs were assembled at Pembina. Now it was over. As the two communities at the two ends of the Red River Trail began to grow into cities, first St. Paul and then Winnipeg, Pembina withered, until the railroad brought the new life of the agricultural frontier to the community. In the 1880s, there was even a famous shootout in town. A man named Bill Collins came to Pembina, taking a job as a bartender at White's Saloon, up on the border. Collins had grown up in Texas, where one of his childhood friends was a fellow named Bill Anderson. Collins and Anderson went to school together and remained friends for a number of years afterward. Collins was the best man at Anderson's wedding, and Anderson had been the best man at Collins'. But eventually the two men drifted apart.

Anderson became a deputy marshal in Texas. Collins moved to Indian Territory, in what became Oklahoma, and took up with a bunch of thieves who specialized in robbing banks and trains. Then, in the late 1870s, Collins and his gang robbed a train near Mesquite, Texas, and most of the gang was captured. Only Collins escaped, and no trace of the cash and gold the gang had stolen was recovered.

Three years later, Texas authorities discovered Collins living in Pembina. Because he had been successful at not getting caught for so long, Collins had sent a letter to his wife, who still lived in Texas. Postal officials intercepted the letter and notified a Texas marshal named Stillwell Russell. When Russell found out about Collins, he sent his deputy, Collins' old friend Bill Anderson, to bring the desperado back to Texas.

Meanwhile, still in Pembina, Collins somehow got wind of the news that Texas authorities were on his trail. By the time Anderson arrived in town, Collins was expecting trouble—though he had no idea the lawman tracking him would turn out to be his old friend. When Anderson arrived, he was met at the train station by Jud LaMoure, who by this time was a deputy marshal. Anderson didn't want to be the one to arrest his old friend, so LaMoure and Pembina County Sheriff Charles

Brown agreed to go to White's Saloon instead, to see if they could get the drop on Collins and make a clean arrest.

But Collins was wary. He talked to the lawmen in a friendly fashion and served them drinks, but he seemed nervous and never turned his back on either man. Brown and LaMoure were well aware of the gun Collins carried and soon decided that Anderson would have to arrest his own criminal. After all, Collins had committed no crime in Pembina.

That left Anderson no choice but to arrest Collins himself. He asked LaMoure and Brown about Collins' daily activities and normal routines. Discovering that his old friend would probably show up at the Pembina post office the next day, Anderson decided to wait there to make the arrest.

Late the next afternoon, as Anderson lay on a bench in the post office lobby, Charles Cavileer, the postmaster, looked out the window and saw Collins coming. "Here comes your man," Cavileer is said to have called to the deputy marshal. When Collins came in, Anderson was waiting for him, with his pistol drawn.

Nobody ever said if Collins looked surprised to see his old friend. As he faced the barrel of the deputy marshal's gun, though, Collins noticed that Anderson was wearing the cufflinks he had given him for a wedding present back in Texas. The men started to talk. Collins mentioned the cufflinks, and a moment later, he went for his gun.

The story of the shooting has circulated in the town for well over a century, preserved for decades by members of the community who were there, including a group of young boys hiding in a nearby stairway while the weapons were firing.

When Collins went for his gun, Anderson shot, hitting his old friend in the hand and chest. At almost the same time, Collins' gun came up and fired at Anderson, who dived through the back door of the post office to get out of the way of any further shooting. Collins positioned himself to get a clear view of the doorway and then, just as Anderson pointed his gun inside to get off another shot, Collins nailed the deputy marshal through the heart at close range.

As the fatally wounded Texan fell to the street, Charles Cavileer sprang from behind the counter and shoved Collins through the open door, knocking him to the ground outside. The former train robber took one last gasp of air and died in the dirt next to his old friend.

Collins' body was buried in an unmarked grave in the Pembina cemetery. For months after the shooting, people said the money from the Mesquite Train Robbery was hidden nearby, perhaps somewhere along the Red River Trail leading into town. Several people dug in what they thought were likely spots, but nobody ever found any treasure in Pembina or on the trail out of town.

Chapter Twelve

Pig's Eye Parrant and the Founding of St. Paul

Historians say that St. Paul was founded in 1837 by Pierre Parrant, although almost nobody called him by that name. Before arriving in Minnesota, some denizen of the prairies had poked out one his eyes, giving him what appeared to be a distinctly porcine squint. After that, he was universally known as "Pig's Eye" Parrant.

Pig's Eye had a varied career as a Métis hunter, trapper and trader, but by the time he arrived on the upper Mississippi, he had settled into whiskey dispensing, perhaps not a time-honored occupation but certainly an age-old specialty market on the North American frontier. Pig's Eye was said to have been born at Sault Ste. Marie, but he worked as a trapper and trader all over the Northwest. For a few years, he worked for the American Fur Company on the Missouri River. He also spent some time in St. Louis. Like others in the fur trade, Parrant discovered somewhere along the way that if you were going to be a frontier trader, it was probably most profitable to sell whiskey.

About 1832, after doing brisk but officially unsanctioned business at a variety of frontier outposts, Pig's Eye Parrant showed up at Fort Snelling. For Parrant, business in the little community that had grown up on the military base around the fort surpassed anything he had seen anywhere else in his long, if undistinguished, career as a dispenser of distilled spirits. His customers were the settlers who lived near the fort and the soldiers who were always anxious to give up a chunk of their paychecks for a good drink (or even a bad one). There were also several nearby Native communities with willing buyers, as well as regular visits from the drivers of ox-cart teams carrying a bit of cash to spend after a few weeks in the wilderness on the Red River Trail.

Officials booted Pig's Eye off the military reservation at Fort Snelling several times during the 1830s because of his whiskey selling, particularly to Native people. The Indian agent there, Major Lawrence Taliaferro, ordered him, in 1835, to stay out of Indian Territory, everywhere in the region, "in any capacity." If Parrant didn't stay away, Taliaferro told him, a military force would be sent after him, and he would be hauled off to Prairie du Chien for trial.

Pig's Eye cultivated an even lower profile after that, but he didn't leave until sometime in 1837. Then, about the time a treaty was negotiated with the Sioux and Ojibwa to give up their land east of the Mississippi, he saw an opportunity. Long before the treaty could be ratified by the United States Senate, Parrant moved across the river and staked the first claim in what was to become the new city of St. Paul, at a spot down-stream from Fort Snelling, just beyond what he thought would be the borders of the military base.

Here, Parrant built a log shack, to serve both as his habitation and as a saloon, of sorts, near Fountain Cave. Pig's Eye's customers had no trouble getting to his new location by the river, and business was easier beyond the borders of the military base. Later, it was noted that while Minneapolis had been founded because of its water power, St. Paul got a liquid start with whiskey.

This observation prompted Mark Twain, after visiting Minnesota some years later, to note: "How solemn and beautiful is the thought that the earliest pioneer of civilization…is never the steamboat, never the railroad, never the newspaper, never the Sabbath School, but always whiskey. The missionary comes after the whiskey—I mean he arrives after the whiskey has arrived."

In 1838, a few others followed Pig's Eye to the east side of the Mississippi, hoping to get in at the beginning of a new settlement. Some were former Red River settlers who had been living on the military base at Fort Snelling—people who had been told to leave because other land was available in the area. Several ex-soldiers, too, moved across the river to settle near Parrant.

In 1840, the last of the settlers on the Fort Snelling land were expelled from their homes, as well as a small group, including Pig's Eye Parrant and Pierre Bottineau, who had built on what turned out to be expanded military property on the east side of the river. These people had already moved downstream to claim home sites at spots they thought, mistakenly, were beyond the military base. But the expulsion in 1840 included additional land on the east side of the river that the army decided it wanted in order to create a larger buffer between the fort and Pig's Eye. They wanted to force the old whiskey trader as far downstream as possible.

By this time, the community growing up near Pig's Eye had taken his name. But naming the new community "Pig's Eye" turned out to be a short-lived honor for him. Responsible folks, particularly the new priests, decided the future city's official designation should be something more dignified, more worthy of respect, so they chose "St. Paul," commemorating the name of the settlement's new log-cabin Catholic mission rather than the veteran whiskey trader. Poor Pig's Eye, who had built the first house and the first business in what would become the Minnesota capital, lost his chance at lasting fame when people switched the name of the new settlement. For several years, the unofficial designation of Pig's Eye carried on for a St. Paul neighborhood, but it, too, gradually fell from use.

When Pierre Bottineau was forced to move farther downstream with Pig's Eye, several other members of his family were also on the upper Mississippi, including his three brothers, Charles II, Basil and Severe, along with their Ojibwa mother, Marguerite. At least one half-brother, a half-sister and a brother-in-law were also there, and perhaps, another brother, too.

Pierre had married Genevieve LaRonce in 1836. Two sons, Pierre and Jean Baptiste were born, and then after the young Pierre died in infancy, a third son was given the same name in 1841. After Genevieve's death in 1851, Bottineau went on to marry Martha Gervais, and between his two marriages, he fathered 26 children, several of whom failed to survive childhood.

After Bottineau settled in St. Paul, he worked at an astounding array of undertakings, including trading independently from his home in what is today the heart of the old downtown. Liquor was probably part of the early trade. One account of him at that time, told in later years by a woman who spent her childhood in early St. Paul, recalls a line of Native people going to "parties" at the Bottineau home.

Pig's Eye, meanwhile, had come upon bigger troubles. After being pushed farther downstream to a new claim, he found himself unable to pay a small debt, apparently about $10, and he somehow lost the claim to the new property he had acquired. After this mishap, he made another claim, and then moved to still another, but around 1844, Pig's Eye abandoned St. Paul for good, after one final defeat on the upper Mississippi.

Pig's Eye, by this time, had been reduced to living on what was just a small lot some distance from his original claim. Here, the city's founder became entangled in a dispute over a property line with his next-door neighbor, a Red River Métis named Michel LeClaire. When the matter finally went before a justice of the peace, it was decided that both properties had been improperly staked. Consequently, the judge said, neither party had a right to either parcel of land.

The hearing took place eight miles from home, but both Pig's Eye and LeClaire started out on foot in a race to be the first back to the disputed property. Pig's Eye was in good shape for an old guy, probably nearing 70, but in the end, he couldn't keep up with LeClaire, who arrived home first and correctly staked his property, to his own advantage. Pig's Eye, forced to live in reduced circumstances, departed from St. Paul soon afterward. There are conflicting reports as to where he moved next. Some say he headed for Sault Ste. Marie but died along the way. Others say he left on the Red River Trail, bound for Manitoba, but no record of him could be found at that location either.

St. Paul, on the other hand, thrived. After the first settlers claimed land at Pig's Eye, the settlement that became known as St. Paul grew slowly but steadily through the 1840s. At the beginning of 1839, when Pierre Bottineau still had a place to live inside what turned out to be the boundaries of the Fort Snelling military base, only about 10 log cabins were on the east side of the Mississippi, in what would eventually become St. Paul. A decade later, when Congress created Minnesota Territory, with St. Paul as the capital, the frontier community was home to at least 700 people.

Over the next year, the population doubled, and after that, it and Minnesota grew faster, with 170,000 people in the territory a decade later, with 10,000 of them living in St. Paul. Even in the 1840s, when the earliest independent merchants started to arrive from outside the region, they began to compete for furs with Henry Sibley and the remnants of the old American Fur Company. And most of the furs they competed for came in on the Red River Trail. Once territorial status was achieved, local commerce expanded with the increasing population. Optimistic new merchants arrived in St. Paul in 1849 confident of Minnesota's future. Wisconsin had become a state in 1848, Iowa two years before that, so the new territory of Minnesota, people believed, would soon follow the same path.

Chapter Thirteen

The Trail to St. Paul

Pig's Eye Parrant and subsequent settlers in St. Paul boosted trade and travel on the Red River Trail as the new community grew, in much the same way that trade grew with the coming of the Woods Trail and Norman Kittson's fur post at Pembina. When the new trail between Crow Wing and Pembina came into use in 1844, it shortened the eastern branch of the Red River Trail and added insurance that the route to St. Paul could be covered on at least one side of the Red River free from interference from the Sioux. Meanwhile, the trail on the west side of the Red grew shorter as well, as cart drivers gradually found shortcuts, eliminated unnecessary meanders and developed a more direct pathway southeast to St. Paul.

In the beginning, the Red River Trail followed the Red and Minnesota rivers, no matter what side of the Red River was initially taken from the settlement. The two branches, east and west, met near the headwaters of the Red and merged for the last half of the trip along the Minnesota Valley to the Mississippi. But the original trail along the Minnesota fell out of favor as the two newer routes created shorter, more distinct trails between Red River and the upper Mississippi.

The Plains Trail skirted the eastern edge of North Dakota along the western side of the valley, crossing the Red

THE TRAIL TO ST. PAUL

River into Minnesota near today's Wahpeton, North Dakota, though there were also alternate crossing points just to the north and south. Once on the east side of the Red, routes developed that led southeast to the mouth of the Sauk River along a path something akin to today's Interstate 94. Near the rapids at the mouth of the river, the trail crossed to the east side of the Mississippi and continued in a southerly direction along that river for another 75 miles until it reached St. Paul.

The shorter Woods Trail was most active during dry summers and autumns or in winter. The cart drivers followed the east trail south from Manitoba more or less paralleling today's Highway 59 as far as Detroit Lakes. The trail then turned sharply to the southeast, into a generally wooded country leading to Crow Wing, where it followed the east side of the Mississippi until it joined the Plains Trail coming in from the west for the final leg of the journey to St. Paul.

When the conditions were right, the Woods Trail was faster than the Plains Trail. And the trail over the gravel ridges on the east side of the Red River were generally dependable, except in the worst weather, with plenty of wood for campfires on or near the trail. By the time the Woods Trail was established, most of the cart drivers had long since abandoned the original trail along the Minnesota River, though it continued to be used locally by traders doing business in and near the valley, and for a while drovers from Red River still took cattle overland to Fort Snelling that way.

For the most part, only Norman Kittson at Pembina persisted with cart caravans from the north on the southern trail into the 1840s, and he stayed with the original route only because of smaller fur posts where, for a short time more, he collected additional pelts along the way. Cart drivers said he liked the old trail because they went only as far as Traverse de Sioux, where Kittson would load the furs onto boats and take them the rest of the way to St. Paul on the water. The cart drivers, meanwhile, waited for his return with trade goods to take north instead of enjoying a celebration in the growing city downriver.

After Kittson shifted his responsibilities entirely to Pembina, he, too, abandoned the original branch of the trail that had opened trade between Red River and the upper Mississippi. Although Kittson was certainly one of the savviest men in the fur business, not all of his success at Pembina was a matter of his prowess as a trader.

Red River had grown by the 1840s. And for the people who lived there, the Hudson's Bay Company and its monopoly seemed less credible than ever. Peter Garrioch wrote in his diary, in 1845, that the Hudson's Bay Company charter "wasn't worth the paper it was written on." Kittson's post at Pembina provided the people of Red River with an easy way around company rules and a needed access point to the rest of the world. Others were willing to fill that role, as well.

It is unknown whether Pierre Bottineau had any particularly favorite route for the trail. There are accounts of him on all of its branches. The route along the Red and Minnesota valleys had been a natural pathway for the original Red River Trail. With the headwaters of two rivers so close, it is easy to believe that, long before the founding of a settlement at Red River, Aboriginal people would have naturally followed the route to trade with each other across the Continental Divide.

The first trader of European background to use the original route with any regularity was probably Robert Dickson, the fur trader who led Thomas Douglas south along the Red and Minnesota rivers in 1817 and then helped establish the Columbia Fur Company. Dickson was a tall, red-headed Scotsman who immigrated to Canada sometime in his youth. As a teenager, he joined the fur trade, and in 1797 he established a post at Lake Traverse on the headwaters of the Red.

The trading area Dickson opened would have been one of the most distant in what was to become the American West, though at the time he arrived, it was a little-known spot that had been variously claimed by England, France and Spain. Another six years would go by before Thomas Jefferson negotiated the Louisiana Purchase for the United States, but even then, there would be some question about whether the area was in British or American territory. The explorers Lewis and Clark, on their famous trek across the American portion of the continent between 1804 and 1806, ran into several traders employed by the North West Company, and a couple who may have been working for Dickson, one of whom may have been his son.

During the War of 1812, Robert Dickson commanded a troop of Sioux and Ojibwa, along with warriors from other tribes, who fought on the British side against the Americans. As was typical in the fur trade, however, his loyalties shifted back and forth as convenience demanded. For a time, he was an American justice of the peace at Prairie du Chien. Over the years, he worked for the North West Company, the American Fur Company and the Hudson's Bay Company, transferring

loyalties between Britain, Canada and the United States when-
ever it seemed necessary or convenient. As an independent
trader, he followed the trail regularly, in both directions, from
Lake Traverse north to Red River and southeast to the upper
Mississippi. He died in 1822, soon after the founding of the
Columbia Fur Company.

Despite Dickson's death, the fur company he helped
create sparked more trade on the Red River Trail than before.
The Columbia's post on Lake Traverse, near the halfway point
of the trail, was a supply point for satellite fur posts as far west
as the Missouri, posts whose trading territory extended north
into Canada. While the trail to Pembina and Red River was
used regularly, it was the section between Lake Traverse and
the Mississippi that was crucial for the company to supply its
other posts, and the Columbia expanded its use of Red River
carts in the process, much the way the Hudson's Bay Company
would a few years later on Canadian trails.

After the American Fur Company bought out the
Columbia in 1827, the new owners continued many of the same
practices the former company had used in the region as the Red
River settlement grew and trade on the trail increased. In the
initial years, it seemed more goods went north on the trail to
Red River than came south. Cattle were driven up the trail regularly in the 1820s. At least one large band of sheep was sent
north in what turned out to be a nearly disastrous attempt by
Selkirk's settlers to begin wool production in the colony.

To obtain the beginnings of a sheep and wool industry,
a group of men went south from Red River to Missouri, where
they passed up what they deemed expensive sheep. They continued their journey east into Kentucky, where they found

ewes at what they considered fair prices. As it turned out, the men should have bought the more expensive animals in Missouri, where the sheep were closer to Red River. In Kentucky, they started a herd of nearly 1400 animals north in May, but before they had gone 100 miles, the sheep began to die, beset by troubles ranging from sore feet to rattlesnake bites.

The worst of it started after the herders crossed the Mississippi. The trouble came from spear grass that grew along the way. Individually, the barbed spears attached to the grass's seed pods seemed harmless, but with thousands of ripened seeds twisting deep into the sheep's wool, the animals were soon beset with small flesh wounds that attracted flies. Before the would-be shepherds knew what was happening, they found their sheep plagued with flesh-eating maggots. The sheep became weaker as they moved north, with more dying each day. By the time the remnants of the herd made it to Manitoba, in the middle of September, more than 1000 sheep had perished on the trail. At the time, there was little consolation found at Red River in the fact that the 241 survivors provided the foundation stock for sheep ranching at the settlement.

By 1835, a regular trade "in horned cattle, horses, furs and some articles of colonial industry" from Red River had become routine going south on the trail. Cattle at Red River had multiplied to numbers that more than met local needs. So for nearly another generation, sending animals down the trail provided the only profitable outlet for surplus animals.

Still, the cattle trade never became as lucrative as the trade of horses. At Red River, cattle herds were of poor quality when they first came up the trail, and they deteriorated rapidly afterward because the animals fed and bred indiscriminately on an open range west of the colony. Horses, on the other hand, used for transportation and hunting, were raised more seriously and most were more carefully bred. Good horses were always in demand at Red River and almost everywhere between the Mississippi and the South Saskatchewan rivers.

Trade along the Red River trail seemed to boom for Pierre Bottineau and others in the late 1830s around the time of the founding of St. Paul. On the west side of the Mississippi, in what was still Native land, commerce was limited to dealings with what was left of the American Fur Company and its loosely aligned cadre of associated traders. East of the river, commerce of all kinds came into being, unimpeded by government regulations.

The trail itself, with two, shorter branches, had become faster than the old trail, and some of the hostility between Sioux and Métis could be avoided. Although the army at Fort Snelling ceaselessly counseled against violence, Sioux flareups, aimed mostly at the Ojibwa but sometimes at the Métis on the trail, had always been a problem. No permission from the Sioux had ever been given to use the trail. (None had been obtained from the Ojibwa for other sections of the trail either.)

All through the 1830s, tensions between the Sioux and the people from Red River increased, culminating when the American Fur Company post at Lake Traverse fell to a Sioux raid and a trader was killed. No matter what branch of the trail they were on, Métis cart drivers kept their guns loaded and close, a habit that was especially important on the journey down the west side of the Red River or when they happened to be on the trail's original route along the Minnesota River Valley.

Even Norman Kittson shifted to the new trail when his business allowed it. Born in Lower Canada, his family members had been in the fur business going back to the first Alexander Henry, a prominent trader in the 1700s. He was the uncle of the Alexander Henry who had been a partner in the North West Company and whose journals recorded life in early Pembina. As a teenager, Kittson took a job with the American Fur Company. After being a thorn in the side of the Hudson's Bay Company for years, he went to work for the British firm as its representative in St. Paul. He was also involved for a short time in the building of the Canadian Pacific Railroad. His son, claiming Canadian birth at "North Pembina," became a member of the Manitoba Legislature.

Although Kittson did business with some of Red River's biggest independent traders, he was not without competition at his Pembina fur post, from both the Hudson's Bay Company and an increasing number of free traders. The opportunities for free traders, it seemed, expanded along with the settlement at Red River. Some went into business on the south side of the international line every year, claiming a Métis birthright to live and trade on whichever side of the border they chose. The Hudson's Bay Company tried to thwart the efforts of both Kittson and the independent traders, but nothing seemed to work.

Everything the company did to punish the independent traders seemed to backfire. When the company shut off special treatment for what it called its petty traders, the traders took their business to the Americans. Later, the company tried raising tariffs on imported goods, but duties did no good because most of the independent traders smuggled goods into Red River anyway. And the Métis at Red River became so angry over the announced increase in duties that the company quietly reduced them again rather than provoke any additional reaction.

Kittson's post at Pembina was ideally situated to trade or sell American goods to anyone at Red River who wanted them. At the same time, Kittson bought furs from any Red River smuggler who made it across the border. In fact, Kittson's location was so good that independent traders from the north regularly moved surreptitiously across the line to compete with him for the Canadian trade. Others, like Bottineau's brother Charles, came north from the upper Mississippi to do the same thing.

Other difficulties, too, regularly disrupted Kittson's activities at Pembina. For two seasons, in 1849 and 1850, when no game seemed to be left in the region, many of Kittson's Native hunters would have starved, he said, if he hadn't extended additional credit for food and supplies. Trade from the north continued to expand, but net revenue went down with the ever increasing competition. Kittson did what he could to keep expenses down, and he eventually abolished credit, switching to a cash-only business. Both measures stimulated more dependable profits, but already it was becoming clear to Kittson that the fur business was in decline and that the boom years were over.

In the 1850s, Kittson, always a businessman first, began to look beyond the immediate returns of the local fur trade. His old friend in the fur business, Henry Sibley, had already abandoned the business. On top of everything else, by that time Pembina appeared destined to be only a minor player in the regional fur economy in favor of Winnipeg just to the north, so Kittson began to act accordingly.

He moved his fur post a few miles west to St. Joseph, a place on the Red River Trail at today's Walhalla where he was out of the Red River flood plain. Once the Hudson's Bay Company stopped trying to enforce its monopoly, in 1849, more trade in St. Paul came down the trail directly from the Canadian side of the border, where the number of independent traders continued to expand. As a result, Kittson turned to business dealings in the growing communities of Winnipeg and St. Paul, the latter a place where he had owned property next to Pierre Bottineau in the early days of the settlement. By 1856, he was already living full time in the Minnesota capital, where he had also been elected mayor.

By that time, St. Paul, with its trail to Red River, had become the commercial capital of Minnesota, and in many ways, Manitoba as well. After the territorial government was established in 1849, settlers poured in from their former homes in Michigan and Wisconsin. Some came all the way from eastern Canada and New England, others from Europe. Many still came down the trail from Red River, but in the 1850s, almost for the first time, immigrants started going north on the trail as well.

Pierre Bottineau had carried out local trading ventures from his home almost as if it were an inn and store since first coming to the upper Mississippi. One early St. Anthony settler named Caleb Dorr tells of visiting the Bottineau home when it was filled with Red River cart drivers spending the night drinking and dancing. Every home Bottineau lived in seemed to be a meeting place for neighbors, travelers, friends or traders. One of his grandchildren said that at the Bottineau home in Red Lake Falls, there always seemed to be room at her grandparents' table for anyone who turned up to eat.

In 1851, Bottineau guided the first railroad survey to cross the northern United States when Isaac Stevens, the new governor of Washington Territory, wanted to start west on the Red River Trail and look for a possible path for the Northern Pacific Railroad on the way. A West Point graduate, Stevens had resigned his army commission that year to become the first governor of the new territory. He took on the job of proposing a feasible rail link across the top of the country since he going that way anyway. Bottineau, Stevens said in a letter to his wife, was the "great guide and voyageur of Minnesota.... Not only is he experienced in all the vicissitudes of travel and frontier life, being the hero of many interesting events, but he has the broadness of view of an engineer, and I am confident he will be of the greatest service to us in finding our way."

Stevens seemed to have a lot of good things to say about Bottineau, praising him in personal correspondence all through the trip and writing a letter of commendation after completing his work with the expedition. His first meeting with Bottineau seems to have gotten the two men off to a good start.

Stevens arrived at the Bottineau home to enlist his guide on a Sunday morning, just in time to join a crowd of people about to consume a large breakfast that included eggs, beefsteak and two suckling pigs. Family members present at the time, Stevens said, included Bottineau's wife, their infant, four children by his first wife, Bottineau's Ojibwa mother, his brother and sister-in-law and another sister-in-law. Everyone, he said, showed great respect toward Bottineau and "in his family I saw exhibited the most refined and courteous manners...."

The railroad surveying trip got underway the same afternoon as Stevens' breakfast at the Bottineau residence, and Stevens wrote later that he learned more of Bottineau's previous adventures while they were on the trail. The initial leg of the survey through Minnesota and eastern North Dakota essentially followed the Red River Trail.

Although there were several points along the Mississippi suitable for a railroad bridge, Stevens deliberately chose to cross at Sauk Rapids so the survey party could take advantage of the existing route. "The object of the exploration being to determine the question of practicability rather than the best route and the details of locations," he wrote. "I determined to cross the Mississippi at Sauk Rapids, continuing for some time on the Red River Trail, and then move as the information, yet to be collected, should determine."

For the most part, Bottineau led Stevens along the existing trail until they crossed the Sheyenne River in today's North Dakota. At this point, they left the Red River Trail behind and continued the survey west as far as Fort Union, near the junction of the Missouri and Yellowstone rivers, where Bottineau completed his contracted duties as guide, just as a new guide joined the expedition to take Stevens farther west.

It's unknown what Bottineau did immediately after leaving the Stevens party, but he probably went to Red River to visit friends and relatives before returning to the upper Mississippi, something he always seemed to do whenever the situation presented itself. Bottineau's son Jean Baptiste and his brother Charles might also have been at Pembina at this time as well, in addition to other relatives.

Later that fall, after returning to the upper Mississippi, Bottineau was once again on the trail, this time leading a party of English Lords and financiers, potential railroad investors, on a prairie hunting trip, although which branch of the trail he traveled is no longer known.

Chapter Fourteen

James Sinclair and Free Trade

In 1839, one of Red River's most prominent free traders, the English-speaking Métis James Sinclair, took a single train of more than 100 ox-carts from Fort Garry to the upper Mississippi. It was the largest train seen up until that time, although it would not hold the record long. The Red River Trail brought income and wealth to folks in the new settlement at St. Paul and the economic backwater at Red River in equal measure, and the ox-cart caravans grew longer with each passing year.

Sinclair had been educated in Scotland. His father, William Sinclair, who died when James was still a child, was a Scottish Hudson's Bay Company trader who had risen to prominence in the firm. Despite his position, the elder Sinclair's last years with the HBC had been unhappy ones, with the long-time trader enduring a mean-spirited demotion not long before his death. Nevertheless, following the instructions in William's will, the company used part of James' inheritance to send the boy to school in Scotland.

After graduating from the University of Edinburgh in the mid-1820s, James Sinclair returned to North America and went to work for the Hudson's Bay Company at a post on James Bay (despite his late father's wish that that he remain in Europe to study and practice law). After only a year at the northern outpost, Sinclair quit the company in 1827 and moved to Red River, where his mother and other family members lived.

Soon after arriving, Sinclair met Andrew McDermot, who had been a friend of his father's and was already known as the king of the Red River traders. Sinclair arranged to work in secret for the older man, trading among the Métis on both sides of the international boundary and occasionally following the Red River Trail to buy domestic goods in the United States. It's unknown when Sinclair took the trail for the first time, but by the end of the 1820s, he had already made several trips to the upper Mississippi and had probably gone as far south as St. Louis.

Only a few folks at either end of the Red River Trail played as significant a role in the development of the trail or benefited from it as much as Sinclair. The number of independent traders increased steadily at Red River, but Sinclair was one of the most well known and richest of the lot. Probably the only exception would have been his mentor and sometime partner, Andrew McDermot.

Even after quitting the company, Sinclair received support from the Hudson's Bay Company as one of its favored independent traders who worked close to the international boundary. Whenever Sinclair's interests diverged from those of the HBC, however, he went his own way. When the HBC stopped paying him higher prices for furs diverted from the American border, Sinclair almost immediately started trading with the American Fur Company, shipping furs over the Red River Trail to the Mississippi.

From the beginning, he was always more than a fur trader. Just like McDermot, he went into any business where money could be made. Sinclair was involved in retail and freighting businesses at Red River and, almost from his first days in the settlement, trade down the trail in the United States. He was an early cattle dealer in Manitoba, and at times he took part in other business ventures as well. He even shipped trade goods for the Hudson's Bay Company across the plains to fur posts west of Red River.

In 1841, Sinclair contracted with the HBC to lead a group of 23 families from Red River to Oregon Territory, where the company hoped a growing population would bolster the British claim and Hudson's Bay Company interests in the region. As soon as he returned to Red River, he immediately reestablished contacts with American traders. The old American Fur Company had essentially disintegrated in everything but name. Most of its assets were split by several smaller operations, with Henry Sibley the leader of a network of traders in the region.

In 1843, Sinclair joined Sibley and Norman Kittson in the scheme that saw Kittson open his trading post at Pembina. Some reports say it was Sinclair who first suggested to Sibley that the Pembina post be opened, but under the original plan, Sinclair was to have managed the operation for Kittson. When trade goods coming in on the new Woods Trail from Crow Wing still hadn't arrived in November 1844, however, and rumors were circulating that the Sioux had killed Kittson on the southern section of the old trail, Sinclair abandoned the project and left Pembina to deal instead with other business matters at Red River.

The year 1844 was also when the Hudson's Bay Company terminated McDermot's and Sinclair's freighting privileges on company ships sailing between England and York Factory on Hudson Bay. The HBC suspected the men, correctly, of clandestine trade with the Americans, and it cut off their shipping rights, while taking other measures designed to limit trade from the south. Sinclair had been exporting tallow from the Métis hunts and Red River's cattle herds to England, but when the HBC cut off his English trading privileges, it even stopped delivery of the tallow he had on route.

Always ready to fight the Hudson's Bay Company, Sinclair, along with more than 20 other prominent Métis, drew up a letter outlining complaints against the company. He submitted the letter, with its theory of Métis rights of free trade, to the governor of Assiniboia at Red River, Alexander Christie, but Christie said the Métis had no more trading rights than any other British subject. The following year, Sinclair took a second letter detailing Métis trading rights to the British government in London, traveling over the Red River Trail to St. Paul where he then made his way to New York City and caught a sailing ship to England. But no action was taken in London on the new petition, either. Sinclair returned to Red River more disgruntled than ever.

Meanwhile, the Hudson's Bay Company had been involved in a little government lobbying of its own. George Simpson, the company's governor, wrote London in 1844 with news of increased activity by the American army near the international boundary. The Americans had come north briefly that year to put an end to the fighting between the Sioux and Métis on the Dakota plains, but Simpson told the British government the soldiers were there because of the Oregon boundary dispute. According to Simpson, the Americans were scheming to cross the border and take over the Red River country, and the government needed to send troops immediately to prevent it.

Simpson's real reason for requesting the British soldiers, of course, was to protect the border from commerce on the Red River Trail. With Kittson at Pembina, Simpson's concern for British territorial integrity was a self-serving ploy. But it worked. James K. Polk had been elected president in 1844, with his supporters chanting, "Fifty-Four-Forty or Fight." The campaign slogan seemed to signify how far north the American claim to the Pacific Northwest stretched and how far the Americans were willing to go to obtain it. It appeared to American voters, and perhaps the government in London, that the United States was ready to go to war if the British didn't give up territory as far north as Russian Alaska. As a bargaining tool, it worked, with the British essentially giving up their claims in Oregon to accept a "compromise" along the 49th parallel.

For Red River, one result of the American bluster was that more than 350 British troops arrived during the summer of 1846 and stayed for two years. But no American soldiers were there to fight. Most of them were, by this time, off fighting in the Mexican War far to the south, a war that would make Santa Fe part of the United States. Still, for the two years the British army stayed in Manitoba, it appeared to reduce some of the independent fur trade that had been hustling up and down the Red River Trail smuggling goods and skins.

Somewhat surprisingly, however, overall trade on the trail increased while the Red Coats were stationed at Red

River. There was still a good trade in furs on the trail, and with soldiers with cash in their pockets who wanted to buy everything from warmer clothes to imported champagne at Red River, all manner of new products started coming up the trail. For as long as the army stayed in town, there was more valuable freight than ever before on the Red River Trail because the settlement suddenly needed more of almost everything.

There wouldn't even have been enough food at Red River to feed the British troops if it hadn't been for the trail. The Hudson Bay Company itself had to send cart trains south for additional supplies for the soldiers during this time. Although the goods Norman Kittson sold at Pembina were now often paid for with British currency rather than furs, his profits soared while the English troops were in North America. And for independent traders like Sinclair, opportunities for trade in new products on the Red River Trail expanded significantly during this time, even if the fur trade itself stagnated or declined. In fact, with the legal commerce now more lucrative than smuggling furs, both Sinclair and McDermot went back to the legitimate trade, contracting work to supply the Hudson's Bay Company with goods. McDermot, already rich, made more money than ever.

In the fall of 1847, Sinclair left the region for two years when he took two of his daughters south through Crow Wing on the Red River Trail. He had arranged for the girls to attend school at Knox College at Galesburg, Illinois. After seeing his daughters safely to their school, Sinclair, ever the adventurer, traveled to St. Louis. It was a city he had visited before, probably beginning in the 1820s when he first started bringing domestic goods up the trail for McDermot. In St. Louis, he renewed old acquaintances in the fur trade and went to the wedding of a new friend he made there, Ulysses S. Grant. While still in St. Louis, Sinclair got wind of the first reports of the discovery of gold in California in 1848, and he left immediately for the west coast. He didn't return to Red River until late in the winter of 1849, after the troops had left the settlement, but Sinclair, reportedly, was somewhat richer when he returned as a result of his months in the gold fields.

Sinclair's return to the Red River country turned out to be timely. The Hudson's Bay Company, attempting once more to enforce its trading monopoly, arrested four Métis traders who were attempting to take furs to Norman Kittson in Pembina. It was one thing for the Hudson's Bay Company to claim theoretical privilege, but it was another matter for them to try to enforce their laws now that the British troops had gone home. The arrests for smuggling stirred up renewed friction in the settlement, and Sinclair was asked to act as the men's counsel at the 1849 trial.

It became known as the free-trade trial at Red River, and the proceedings unfolded as a classic frontier courtroom scene if ever there was one. Each member of the 12-man jury listened to the proceedings with his rifle in his hand. Norman Kittson's father-in-law, though hardly impartial, was one of the jurors. Meanwhile, a band of 500 well-armed Métis crossed the river and surrounded the log building where the trial took place, making it clear what they intended to do if the court reached a decision they disliked. The Métis protesters, led by Jean-Louis Riel (father of Louis Riel, the man the Canadian

Métis scouts from Red River while working with the International Boundary Commission in the early 1870s.

government would hang 36 years later for leading Métis rebellions in 1870 and 1885), said if the four defendants were sent to jail, they would be forcibly freed. Public opinion was such that the HBC's trade restrictions were about to come to an end no matter what happened to the men that day in court.

When the verdict was read, the four men were found guilty of trading furs in the United States, but the jury recommended that no penalty be imposed because the men claimed, improbably, not to have realized trading south of the border was illegal. The convicted felons were immediately set free. And as they walked from the building, their comrades outside jumped to the conclusion that they had been found innocent. According to legend, Riel shouted, "*Vive la liberte! Le commerce est libre!*"

And the commerce was free; the inconclusive trial was all it took. For the Hudson's Bay Company, there was no going back. Public opinion was too great. The company had to accommodate the Métis and open trade on the Red River Trail. No matter what its charter might say, the HBC monopoly was gone, and the trade war on the Red River Trail was lost. The company immediately made other concessions to the Métis, including permitting the use of the French language during court proceedings and adding Métis representatives to Red River's pathetically meager local government, the Council of Assiniboia. The Hudson's Bay Company avoided taking any action that might offend the sensibilities of what it had finally realized was a predominantly Métis community at Red River.

For James Sinclair, the long fight was not so simply resolved. Despite his wealth, he was discouraged with life at Red River and the constant frustration he felt toward the Hudson's Bay Company. Sinclair presented yet another petition outlining Métis rights to the HBC's governor, George Simpson, and then left for St. Paul late in 1849, where he applied for and was granted United States citizenship.

Like Bottineau and so many others in the fur trade, Sinclair seemed to have one foot on each side of the border. Now, though, he sold his property at Red River and sent his household goods down the Red River Trail to the Mississippi. At St. Paul, he sent his belonging by steamboat to New Orleans. From there, everything was to be shipped around the horn of

South America to Oregon. Sinclair's intention was to lead one more group of emigrants from Red River across the mountains to the West Coast, but this time the settlers were to include his family.

But floods during the spring of 1850 on the Red River foiled his plan, so Sinclair left his family in the settlement and went west alone. When he got to the coast, he discovered that his belongings had been lost in a shipwreck. Sinclair spent the next year and a half in Oregon and California, returning to Red River in 1852, where he reconciled with his on-again, off-again business partner, George Simpson.

The always resourceful Simpson apparently recruited Sinclair in a plan that would rid Red River of several irritating traders prominent on the Red River Trail, along with Sinclair himself. Simpson used Sinclair to induce a few of Simpson's other bothersome competitors to move to the Oregon country, too. To accomplish this feat, Simpson offered Sinclair the salary of a chief trader with the company, plus land and 200 cattle once he got to Oregon. The deal was to remain secret until after the emigrants left Red River. In return, Sinclair became an agent for the company, signing up others to leave on his journey to the Pacific Northwest. Once there, he was promised a continuing job with the company, but in American territory.

As a result, in 1854, Sinclair once more led an emigrant train—including most of his family—from Red River across the mountains to the Oregon country. A little more than a year later, still working for the Hudson's Bay Company, he was killed during a Native uprising. His most lasting contribution to his former community was the role he played in lifting trade barriers and stimulating commerce on the Red River Trail.

Chapter Fifteen

Minnesota Statehood

When the Hudson's Bay Company gave up trying to enforce its trade restrictions on the Red River Trail, it only acknowledged reality: the people of Red River were no longer willing to tolerate the company's limitations on trade. Slowly, the economy was advancing. Immigrants soon came to Manitoba in the same way they had already started to arrive in Minnesota. While the economy at Red River plodded along at what sometimes must have seemed a barely discernible pace, St. Paul boomed. The same year the Hudson's Bay Company grudgingly gave up its monopoly in the fur trade, 1849, Minnesota brought in territorial government. St. Paul became the capital of the newly named Minnesota Territory.

James M. Goodhue, the publisher of Minnesota's first daily newspaper, who had arrived in town four weeks earlier, said in the inaugural issue of the *Minnesota Pioneer* that the city "which was but yesterday unknown, for the reason that it had then no existence" occupied a beautiful site where "bilious fevers and argue did not exist." The speed of new construction was so swift, he said, that a description of the community on that date would be inadequate in a month's time.

Optimistic merchants in St. Paul saw settlers and fortune on the northern horizon. The HBC's contract with the

British government, giving it sovereignty across all of the north that drained into the great Arctic bay, would expire in 1869. Baring an extension, it seemed, a new order would finally come to Red River, politically and economically, bringing with it more settlers and a wealth of new opportunity. And Minnesota, with its rapidly expanding trade on the Red River Trail, would reap some of the benefits.

Goods carried up the trail had already become more than just basic supplies for the fur trade. The trail had always carried some general merchandise to settlers at Red River, along with typical trading goods such as axes, ammunition and beads, but by the 1850s, household items and farm equipment in greater proportions than ever before began moving up the trail. The trail became less and less reliant on the fur trade and more a source of general imports.

Kittson expanded his trade at Pembina right along with the increasing population at Red River. But it was no longer just the Hudson's Bay Company making the Pembina trade difficult for the veteran fur trader. The independent traders around Red River on both sides of the international boundary were also hard at work. Especially after 1849, these small traders in the region became more than just middlemen smuggling goods from Red River to Pembina. More and more, they competed openly with Kittson, buying furs and selling them wherever they could get the best prices, often in St. Paul to merchants who had only recently arrived.

St. Paul's fortunes, of course, were never strictly tied to Kittson's success or failure on the Red River Trail. Kittson, after all, offered only one of several avenues available in the expanding trade with the British Northwest. If he hadn't been at Pembina, some other trader would have picked up much of the same business. Virtually all of Red River's independent traders sold goods that came from or through the Minnesota capital. St. Paul, at the head of navigation for the paddle-wheeled steamboats carrying American commerce from the heart of the continent, appeared destined to become the channel through which all trade with the Red River country flowed.

In the early 1840s, the steamboat business on the upper Mississippi had been primitive. The irregular and undependable schedules and service might have been good enough for the fur trade and for a military fort, but it was inadequate for the frontier community growing at St. Paul. But by the middle of the decade, four or five boats boasted regular schedules running between Prairie du Chien and the upper Mississippi. The summer of 1845 saw 45 steamboats arrive at St. Paul, all carrying goods and people from the south. In 1847, a weekly steamboat from Galena, Illinois, started making scheduled trips, and by the 1850s, boats docked at St. Paul from Illinois three times a week, with daily runs from Prairie du Chien. In winter, stagecoach lines connecting St. Paul to the south made regularly scheduled trips by the middle of the century.

Dependable steamboat service brought St. Paul closer to eastern markets and, somewhat paradoxically, made the Red River Trail more important to the local economy. With better transportation out of St. Paul to the south, the trail became more competitive, until it completely eclipsed the Hudson's Bay Company's old transportation route to England. New merchants in the Minnesota capital looked optimistically to future statehood, but for the local economy, in the early territorial years, it was trade coming from the Red River Trail that provided the largest, most dependable business in the frontier city. One newspaper correspondent in St. Paul wrote that the new city, at the head of river communication, would provide trade for the vast regions north of it, all the way to the Selkirk Settlement.

During the 1840s, caravans of more than a hundred Red River carts took to the trail regularly between the British Northwest and the upper Mississippi. In the 1850s, the caravans grew until the largest each year included 200 carts or more. But the smaller cart trains, too, contributed to the growing commercial center at St. Paul. Not even lumber could rival furs and buffalo hides as a Minnesota export during the territorial years.

Railroad construction, moving steadily westward, brought faster transportation closer. Travel times and the cost of shipping both decreased as they crept nearer to the Minnesota border. And the closer they came, the more profitable trade on the trail grew. More importantly, for those in Manitoba, as the railroads came closer, merchandise coming up the trail became cheaper. The economy of the British Northwest, aligning itself with Minnesota, was emerging from its isolation.

In Minnesota, when the 1850s began, most of the territory outside St. Paul still belonged to the Native people of the region, but almost immediately the government began to negotiate large property cessions from the Sioux and Ojibwa. The first land concessions after territorial status were made by the Sioux when Governor Alexander Ramsey went up

Alexander Ramsey was the first governor of Minnesota Territory and the second governor of the State of Minnesota. He also served on several treaty delegations along with Pierre Bottineau.

the Minnesota River to meet with the Sisseton and Wahpeton Dakota to arrange a treaty that, in 1851, virtually stripped the Natives of their homeland in the Minnesota River Valley. A separate treaty was signed with the Mdewakanton and Wahpekute at Mendota the following month.

Once the Sioux treaties were out of the way, Ramsey hired Pierre Bottineau as his guide and interpreter and, despite the lateness of the season, he headed up the Red River Trail to Pembina with a government delegation to negotiate with the Ojibwa of the Red River Valley, the so-called Pembina Chippewa, along with those at Red Lake. Following a typical route for the time, Bottineau took the West Plains Trail through central Minnesota, along the Sauk River to the Bois de Sioux and then crossed over to the west side of the Red River.

Five days north of the Sheyenne River, the expedition encountered buffalo for the first time, and Bottineau led the men in two days of hunting. On the second day, Bottineau's horse stumbled during the chase, and he was thrown to the ground. Stunned and somewhat insensible from the fall, he nevertheless appeared to have no other wounds so was bled as a means of treatment and put to bed in the back of a wagon.

Nothing more is known of Bottineau's wounds or how long it took him to recover, but apparently he mended relatively fast because he was able to handle his duties during the treaty negotiations a few days later. On the return trip, Bottineau was in good enough humor to play a prank on Ramsey. Somewhere along the way he killed and roasted a skunk, which he presented to the Minnesota governor for supper. He had heard Ramsey brag earlier that he liked skunk meat just fine. Ramsey, however, declined Bottineau's offering, saying that roasted skunk was, indeed, very tasty, at least at those times when he was very hungry, but with only an ordinary hunger, he said, he was unable to tolerate it.

The treaty making at Pembina went well for the government, which essentially demanded the Ojibwa transfer approximately 30 miles of land on each side of the Red River, from the

Canadian boundary to the territory already ceded to the government by the Sioux along the Buffalo River far to the south. In exchange, the government promised to pay the Natives $10,000 per year, for 20 years, though there were also some restrictions that would limit those promises. And of course, traders got first crack at the money for anything they said was owed to them by the Natives. A decade later, the Episcopal bishop in Minnesota, Henry Whipple, said that the only actual negotiations involved with treaty making with Indians were those carried on between the Indian agents, the traders and the politicians. The views of the Indians, themselves, Whipple said, were, unfortunately, of no consequence.

The Ojibwa treaty was in all ways a steal for the government, more lucrative than the Sioux treaties signed earlier in the year, but the United States Senate rejected the treaty negotiated at Pembina. It was a time when divisions between North and South in the United States colored every issue, and the treaty was essentially discarded because Southern senators rejected anything that might strengthen the North. Even the Sioux treaties were amended, because of Southern obstinacy in the upper chamber, in the hope that the Natives would reject the whole works. Somehow, traders convinced the Sioux to go along with the treaty even though no provision for a reservation of land was provided, only a promise that the president would arrange for something unspecified later. The Ojibwa treaty, on the other hand, was thrown out completely, and it would be 12 years before another treaty ceding the Red River Valley was signed. When that time came, Pierre Bottineau once again led the American delegation up the Red River Trail, where he would play an even bigger role in the outcome of the treaty.

Meanwhile, after Minnesota became a territory, the population (which, with forged numbers, probably amounted to less than the required 5000 white residents necessary for territorial status) jumped quickly upward once title for much of the future state had been ceded by the Natives. According to the 1860 census, 175,000 people lived in Minnesota, most of them in communities and homesteads along the Mississippi, Minnesota and St. Croix rivers—with St. Paul taking its place as the commercial and political center for the territory.

The future city's initial settlement had roughly coincided with Kittson and Rolette establishing their trading center at Pembina. Afterward, St. Paul's growth, for clear reasons, corresponded to increased commerce on the Red River Trail. Neither was wholly dependent on the other, but trade with Kittson's post and direct trade with the increasingly important Red River free traders brought clear economic returns for St. Paul and Minnesota at a time when lumber exports were small and agricultural production was still mostly a promise for the future. Merchants in St. Paul looked forward optimistically to statehood and long-term fortune, but in 1850, and for some time to come, the Minnesota economy stayed tied to trade in Canadian furs and prairie buffalo hides.

In the 1850s and 1860s, St. Paul's fur trade was the second largest in the U.S., behind only St. Louis. But at least 80 percent of that trade, and probably more, was brought into the country from the Canadian West on the Red River Trail. Métis cart drivers, who first glimpsed St. Paul when Pig's Eye sold whiskey there, were still loading Red River carts bound for a state capital a generation later.

Pierre Bottineau probably made trips up and down the Red River Trail almost yearly well into the 1840s, and he continued to make the trip for one reason or another on a fairly regular basis after that. Real-estate speculation seemed an early preoccupation in Minnesota, and Bottineau joined in enthusiastically from the beginning, first in St. Paul and then in St. Anthony Falls. Around 1845, he sold the last of his land in downtown St. Paul, though according to some reports he made only a small profit on the $300 sale. By this time, Bottineau had already moved to St. Anthony, where he had built a house on land that included much of the east bank of the river near the falls. He also owned part of Nicollet Island.

His new home in St. Anthony, probably the second frame house inside the boundaries of what became the city of Minneapolis (the town of St. Anthony Falls was annexed to Minneapolis in 1872), undoubtedly would have been more convenient for him than staying in St. Paul because of his work on the river and trail. The St. Anthony location was probably a good real-estate bet, as well, and it was a place where he'd be able to continue with his trading ventures.

The year after Bottineau sold his St. Paul claim, he sold a piece of his St. Anthony property for $500, which was $350 more than he had originally invested in the entire parcel, so it looked as if the real-estate venture might pay off. In 1849, he hired a future Minnesota governor, W.R. Marshall, to survey his St. Anthony property so he could begin selling lots in the new community. Bottineau, who had spent his life in the wilderness and on the open plains, evidently had no trouble understanding that things would soon change around the falls on the

Mississippi. And he apparently meant to profit when they did. The same year the property was surveyed, he began selling lots in what became known as Bottineau's Addition. Later, he invested in a ferry at a point farther north on the Mississippi.

According to most accounts, however, Bottineau was seldom a particularly good businessman, so he seems to have missed his chance for a real-estate empire at St. Anthony. He acquired a lot of promise-to-pay notes, but little in the way of cash for his city lots. At this point in his life, Bottineau was as well known for his financial profligacy as for his real-estate savvy or wilderness exploits. According to legend, he sat at a poker table holding three queens, but lost his Nicollet Island property in the card game.

Another story had it that he sometimes entertained local children by skipping silver dollars across the Mississippi River. On yet another occasion, sometime later, Bottineau was fined 10 dollars for riding a horse too fast across a new bridge spanning the Mississippi at Minneapolis. He cheerfully handed the justice of the peace a 20-dollar gold piece, twice what was required. "Take it," he said. "I'll be going back just as fast." About this time he also picked up the nickname "Richee" Bottineau for his free and easy ways with money.

Bottineau advertised in the new St. Anthony newspaper, in 1851, that he had land for sale, with lots and acreages "cheap for cash," as well as several pieces of farm equipment at good prices. Other newspaper advertisements in Minnesota at the time included ones for several river ferries, such as the one at Sauk Rapids "on the road to Red River" and another at Crow Wing that aided travelers on the trail to "Selkirk's Colony."

In April 1851, Bottineau's wife, Genevieve, died at their home near the falls. Gauging by the previous census, a year earlier, the Bottineaus probably had six children living at the time. Infant twins, Leon and Elsie, had died just a few months before their mother. In addition, Bottineau's aging mother would also have been a member of the household, along with other relatives and occasional overnight guests passing through town.

A few months after the death of his wife, Bottineau took on the job of guiding Governor Alexander Ramsey on his treaty-making expedition up the Red River Trail to negotiate with the Ojibwa. After the negotiations, he took Ramsey farther north for a short visit to Red River, which also gave Bottineau a chance to visit relatives and his 12-year-old daughter, Marie, who attended a school run by the Grey Nuns at St. Boniface. In January 1852, Bottineau married Martha Gervais, the daughter of a Red River family who had lived on the upper Mississippi for more than a decade.

Despite his profligacy, Bottineau was moderately successful with real estate at St. Anthony Falls and still more successful as a trader with the Natives, which probably encouraged him to buy the inn and trading post at Elk River in 1849. He still took on occasional freighting contracts on the Mississippi River above St. Anthony Falls, and perhaps more importantly, he continued to sign up for guiding opportunities as they presented themselves.

Bottineau built a new inn and trading post at Elk River to replace his old one in 1850. In 1854, he filed a claim on property at what became known as "Bottineau Prairie" near today's

Osseo, Minnesota, an area he had occasionally traveled through for several years, going between St. Anthony and his inn at Elk River. Soon, he started selling town lots at this new location, built a new house for his family and took up farming.

At St. Anthony, Bottineau was one of the first to arrive in a new settlement, but he didn't gain substantial wealth from the developing city of Minneapolis before leaving. He did, however, keep the St. Anthony house for a few more years, probably in some kind of business arrangement that allowed trading activities to continue from the building.

Bottineau had done essentially the same thing in St. Paul, moving on from a developing city to the fringes of the settlements before the property he owned appreciated significantly. Unlike St. Anthony or St. Paul, Bottineau stayed at Osseo for more than 20 years before moving on. This was probably because his farm there remained on the rural fringes rather than in the heart of the developing metropolis.

Bottineau was once more taking part in the real-estate boom in territorial Minnesota at Osseo, but the move also suited his personal needs better, and as such it was something more than economic speculation. Just as he moved to St. Anthony when St. Paul began to grow larger, as soon as people started to get too numerous in St. Anthony, he escaped to the nearby countryside at Osseo.

And Bottineau wasn't alone in his desire to escape Minnesota's developing urban population. Just as several French-speaking Métis had followed him to St. Anthony, a number of families also followed Bottineau to Osseo. These were generally people he had known all his life, first at Red River, then later in

St. Paul. At Osseo, they included, among others, members of his new wife's family, as well as Antoine LeCompte, the son of Bottineau's wilderness mentor who had been shot and killed by Thomas Simpson in 1840 on the Red River Trail. Bottineau's brother, Severe, also homesteaded at Osseo.

But settlement and civilization was coming to Bottineau Prairie, too, and the rest of Minnesota. In the winter of 1857, Bottineau and his brother Charles guided a group of about eight land speculators part way up the Red River Trail. Their plans were to take out claims at what would one day become the town of Breckenridge, Minnesota. At the time, although railroad mania was at a fever pitch in the territory, the railroad, itself, had yet to establish a beachhead beyond the Mississippi. Train tracks would not reach the Red River for more than a decade, making the time much too far off for anyone to make money that year surveying potential town sites in the remote Red River Valley. But optimism was in the air, and Bottineau led his group of speculators up the trail in early January to get a head start on what the speculators assumed would be a rush of land-hungry settlers in the spring.

Snowstorms punctuated the first few days of the expedition, so that by the end of the first week the men, with two sleighs, five yoke of oxen and an Indian pony, were trudging through snowdrifts three and four feet deep, "with no sign of a road in sight," according to George Dailey, one of the speculators. Camped near a homestead a few nights later, Dailey said, he was sitting with Bottineau next to the campfire in the dark when they saw a boy about 12 years old coming toward them. According to Dailey, Bottineau whispered that he was going to scare the boy. As the kid got closer, Bottineau took out his hunting knife and leaped over the fire "letting out a wild Indian yell that made the woods ring." The boy, according to the story, retreated at a run.

A few days later, a blizzard blew in on the trail and Bottineau ordered everyone to bed, huddled together under buffalo skins and comforters. About three o'clock the following morning, Dailey said, after a miserable night with little sleep, he woke up when he heard Bottineau building a campfire and singing a song in Ojibwa. When he crawled from underneath the robes, he went to the fire and asked the guide what he was singing about. Bottineau told him it was a song of encouragement for difficult times.

After the expedition finally reached the Red River at the end of January, Bottineau returned to St. Anthony, leaving his charges to lay out lots at what would one day become the town of Breckenridge. They would also make claims at what they hoped would be other nearby town sites. The following summer, however, Bottineau returned to the Red River and made yet another nearby claim on a proposed town site called Dakota City, located near the mouth of the Sheyenne River on the west bank of the Red, at what he guessed would be the head of steamboat navigation on the river.

No actual income came to Bottineau from any of the town site speculation, however, except the money he earned as a guide, mostly because the Panic of 1857 popped Minnesota's real-estate bubble within weeks of his staking his claims at Dakota City. The panic, which came about with a too expansive economy, was followed by a financial depression that put a damper on the Minnesota economy until after the end of the Civil War. Steamboats began running on the Red River in 1859, but railroad construction stalled, and then ran out of steam just as Minnesota territory was about to become a state.

Just before the recession began, delegates had gathered to write a state constitution. And, anticipating statehood, people went to the polls soon afterward to elect a governor and legislature. One-time fur-trader Henry H. Sibley led the Democrats to a narrow victory in the election, beating the Republican nominee, Alexander Ramsey, in the contest for governor.

But a deadlock in Congress, again over the slavery issue, delayed statehood until May 1858. Even so, Minnesota's political progress came relatively fast, at least compared to the stagnation gripping the northern end of the Red River Trail. In 1849, the same year Minnesota became a territory, the Métis at Red River celebrated the coming of free trade, but in the years that followed, while trade between Red River and St. Paul grew, Manitoba continued to be ruled by the Hudson's Bay Company, with its accompanying hostility to the whole notion of settlement. The HBC tolerated the settlers who were there but remained hostile to any changes in their status or any additional settlement. Even with free trade and the diminishing fur economy, the company was large and powerful enough to hang on a while more and increased its profits for two more decades after free trade.

While the economic situation in St. Paul turned from boom to stagnation in the fall of 1857, and was then interrupted by a war-time economy during the Civil War, in the first half of the 1860s, the political situation at Red River mostly dozed. The financial panic and the war that followed helped to extend the life of the Red River Trail a few years longer than would otherwise have been the case. Railroad construction that had moved steadily toward St. Paul and would eventually supplant the trail across Minnesota came almost to a halt during the last two years of the 1850s and hardly moved at all for the next half decade.

The Michigan Southern railroad had reached Chicago in 1852, and work immediately started on a Chicago to Galena line, with a stage line operating between the end of steel and the Mississippi River. In 1854, the Chicago and Rock Island Railroad reached the great river's edge. In 1858, the Chicago and Milwaukee Railroad reached LaCrosse, Wisconsin, a mere 150 miles downstream from St. Paul. But then the new railroads almost completely stopped construction.

Railroad building, despite Bottineau guiding surveyors for the Northern Pacific over a possible route leading to the West Coast in 1853, never got a good start inside Minnesota's borders. Even so, with direct railroad connections in the 1850s from nearby points east of the Mississippi, and existing river transportation from St. Paul on the Mississippi, Minnesota then lay only four days travel from Washington, D.C. Freight between the new state and New York City took a week or less. If there had ever been a question about the Red River Trail being the most practical route for Manitoba commerce, none existed after the new rail lines began to connect the trail to the rest of the world east of the Mississippi.

More than 1000 steamboats docked at the Minnesota capital in 1858 when the Hudson's Bay Company began shipping virtually all of its furs and trade goods on the Red River Trail, adding huge amounts to the goods already going down the trail with the free traders. After fighting the independent traders on the trail for nearly 40 years, the company took up for itself the more economical transportation system to the south. St. Paul had become, for all intents and purposes, Red River's sole connection to the outside world. Manitoba and Minnesota's destiny seemed forever linked.

There had been talk for several years of extending steamboat service to the Red River, and in 1858 the St. Paul Chamber of Commerce offered a $2000 bonus to anyone who could launch and pilot the first steamboat to Fort Garry. During the winter of 1858–59, Anson Northrup, who owned a tiny steamboat for use on the Mississippi between Little Falls and Grand Rapids, dismantled the vessel and, with dozens of oxen and more men, hauled the boat across the frozen lakes and streams along the trail from Crow Wing to the upper Red River near Fort Abercrombie. Once on the Red, he rebuilt the ship and renamed it after himself. Then, early in the summer of 1859, the *Anson Northrup* steamed into Winnipeg, unloaded passengers and goods and returned to Fort Abercrombie, where Northrup docked his boat and headed for St. Paul to collect his reward.

Knowing a good idea when he saw one, HBC governor George Simpson bought the *Anson Northrup* and turned its operation over to James and Henry Burbank, two brothers who were transforming the portion of the Red River Trail from St. Cloud west to the Red River into a stage-coach route. Simpson used the Burbanks' Minnesota Stage Company to hide the Hudson's Bay Company ownership of the steamboat. It seemed like a good plan for both companies, but each had conflicting needs in the business deal, and in the end, things turned sour.

The HBC needed an economical way to ship its own goods between St. Paul and Winnipeg, while at the same time choking off transportation for its rivals and discouraging future development at Red River. The Burbanks, on the other hand, wanted to sell as many stage and steamboat tickets as possible, the more settlers the better. The more freight they shipped, no matter the owners, the better yet.

It was not surprising that conflicts between the Burbanks and Simpson soon emerged. As soon as the unsatisfactory partnership could be ended, Simpson turned to his old nemesis at Pembina, Norman Kittson, and asked him to run his steamboat and look after the rest of the company's interests in the United States.

Although a stage-steamboat connection seemed an obvious replacement for the traditional Red River carts, Simpson wasn't prepared to abandon the idea of the cart caravans entirely, and his notion proved wise in the coming years when the undependable Red River regularly interrupted steamboat schedules. Even in the best of years, river traffic was only open for two or three months in the summer, and most years less than that. Several times before the coming of the railroad, low water kept the steamers off the river all summer long. On these occasions, the Hudson's Bay Company still had the trail to get its goods through. Competing traders used the trails most of the time anyway because the HBC, for the most part, made shipping goods for rivals by steamboat too expensive.

S.H. Scudder, in his book *The Winnipeg Country*, tells of being stranded in Manitoba in 1860. Scudder had been in Rupert's Land with a scientific expedition that had gone north to observe that summer's eclipse of the sun, but when they got back to Winnipeg, they found out the steamboat they had intended to take south to the stage line had run aground on a sandbar just downriver from Fort Garry. No further steamboat traffic took place on the Red River for the rest of the season. It was still a month before a fall cart caravan to St. Paul was planning to leave, so Scudder and his group joined with others who had intended to take the steamboat south and arranged for a separate cart train of their own.

They planned to take the east branch of the trail, through Crow Wing, and for several days, as they tried to get organized for the trip at Red River, more people signed up to come along. The cart train, Scudder said, seemed to increase its size daily. By the time it left Red River for St. Paul, the train included two dozen carts and several small bunches of cattle and ponies that dawdled along for half a mile behind. A dozen mounted Métis rode at the front of the caravan, watching for any signs of the Sioux. A buffalo cow free on the prairie followed along behind, trying to stay close to its calf that someone had caught and tied to the back of one of the carts.

The party went down the west side of the river, but only as far as Pembina, where it crossed over to the east side and then followed the Woods Trail to the Mississippi at Crow Wing. One day was much like another on the trail, something like being in a canoe, Scudder said, except that the weather was never allowed to interfere with the journey. They were always up by daybreak, well before 5:00 AM, so they could put in an hour or two before breakfast. There would be a few more hours of travel as the carts bounced along on the prairie before stopping to let the cattle and horses graze around noon. More miles of trail were put behind them in the afternoon before making camp, sometimes early, but other times late in the evening. No matter when camp was called, however, the train moved on again the next morning soon after dawn.

In the entire distance between Pembina and Crow Wing, Scudder said, the caravan passed through only two settlements large enough to have a name: Leaf City and Wadena. Each boasted one log house. At the Mississippi, the ox pulling the first cart was driven onboard the unsteady ferry to make the crossing to Crow Wing. Once aboard, however, the ox went straight to the front of the boat, where it leaped into the river, pulling its cart, plus another ox and cart tied behind it, into the water as well. Both carts flipped over in the river's current, sending boxes, pails, kegs and barrels floating downstream, while the oxen, pulling their almost empty carts, swam to the opposite shore. Most of the valuable items, including a few bales of furs, Scudder reports, were eventually retrieved from the water.

Throughout the 1860s and 1870s cart trains continued to use the trail. In fact, over most of that time, the volume and value of goods increased from year to year. The value of legally imported goods passing through Pembina to Red River doubled during the Civil War years of 1861 to 1865, and then doubled again, at a time when imported goods were still as likely to be smuggled into the country as not.

If Minnesota's destiny was tied to the Red River settlement, and it was, the old trail could only be completely replaced by the coming of steel rails, which promoters and residents alike assumed would happen soon. In 1859, as Minnesota completed its first year of statehood amid economic and political turmoil in the buildup to the Civil War, most people would have been surprised to learn that a railroad connection to the north was still about two decades away, two decades when the old Red River cart trail would continue to carry people and goods back and forth across vast stretches of wilderness.

Still, the shape of the new state of Minnesota appeared to have been created with Red River in mind. Minnesota Territory had reached from the Mississippi to the Missouri River and north all the way from Nebraska to the Canadian border, but the boundaries were too great and the territory too large to become just one state. Because most of the population lived in the southeast near the Mississippi, a state something akin to Iowa with comparatively short north-to-south borders but reaching west to the Missouri River, would have been logical.

But legislators chose, instead, to create a tall narrow state reaching into the unpopulated north, between the Mississippi and the Red rivers, much of it an empty land where the treaty process hadn't been completed with the Native people. There was, of course, reason in this madness. While there might not be settlers, once the government took care of the Native lands, Minnesota would be a state that could take advantage of a transcontinental railroad from Lake Superior to the Pacific that would connect it with all the trade that might come into the country from Manitoba and the British

Northwest. There was only the problem of extinguishing the remaining land claims held by the state's indigenous people, something in which Pierre Bottineau, with previous treaty-making experience, would play a prominent role.

In the meantime, Bottineau took on a guiding expedition for a wagon train that would retrace some of the route he had taken with Isaac Stevens nearly a decade earlier. In 1862, Captain James Fisk led a contingent of gold seekers west from St. Paul to Idaho, with Bottineau serving as guide for the first half of the trip between the Mississippi and the Yellowstone rivers.

Again, as in the earlier trip, Bottineau began the journey by following the Red River Trail west along the Sauk River. He was paid $100 per month for his services, but Samuel Robert Bond, the secretary for the expedition, wrote in his journal that the guide showed up for work in St. Cloud the day before the wagon train was set to start in an alcoholic drunk, which Bond described in the racially insensitive terms of the time. Bond, apparently, was unimpressed with the new guide, but the next day he rode with Bottineau, along with Bottineau's 15-year-old son, Daniel, from St. Cloud to St. Joseph, where they rejoined Fisk's wagon train. It was during that ride that Bond's opinion of Bottineau began to change for the better.

The day after that, the cart train passed a group of 40 to 50 Red River carts on the way to St. Paul, owned, Bond said, by Bottineau's brother Charles, who lived near Pembina and ran a trading firm there. Charles Bottineau rode what Bond described as a "fine buffalo horse," with beautiful saddle and tack. When Captain Fisk admired the horse, Charles gave it to him before his party moved on toward St. Paul.

Later that day, following the trail toward Alexandria, Bond wrote that after they entered "the big woods," the road became so muddy they had to cut trees to corduroy the trail so the wagons could get through. The following day, Pierre Bottineau took Bond hunting, where he shot 10 ducks and five or six plovers. Bond enjoyed the experience so much he asked Bottineau to take him the next day as well. This time he shot a sandhill crane, 16 more ducks and 12 more plovers.

The day after that, as they neared Breckenridge, Bond said they saw a buffalo on the trail for the first time, and then a war party of Ojibwa riding south looking for Sioux to fight. By July 4, the group had reached Fort Abercrombie, where they took in the Independence Day celebrations. Then, after moving on a few days later, the expedition passed beyond the Sheyenne River, thus leaving the Red River Trail where it continued north to the international boundary. The wagon train headed northwest on what Fisk intended to be the most direct route to their destination on the Salmon River.

On July 14, the train came in sight of a high ridge running north and south that divided the waters of the Sheyenne from those of the Wild Rice River. Captain Fisk named the highest point on the ridge Mount Bottineau. Several in the party climbed the newly named peak and buried a paper listing some of the expedition's particulars under a rock.

By this time, the group had already come across scattered buffalo, and several were killed. The next day, however, they saw what Bond described as the first large herd, and for the next several days they saw more buffalo, with Bottineau and others killing many of them.

On July 21, while Bottineau was off hunting, his horse, Major, tripped in a wolf hole and rolled on top of him. Bond wrote that they carried the fallen guide to one of the wagons with what they feared were serious injuries, but before nightfall Bottineau was horseback again, hunting more buffalo. At the end of the day, Bond estimated they had seen 100,000 buffalo since they had left camp that morning. A few days later, they had to bridge the Mouse River to get the wagons across. Bond noted that everyone worked on the bridge except Bottineau, who had other duties and, more significantly, said he preferred not to work with the other men.

Bottineau stayed with the Fisk expedition until the wagon train reached Fort Union on August 11. At that point, another guide had been contracted to take the expedition farther west. Bottineau shook hands with everyone, Bond said, "and was much affected at the regret all evinced on his leaving." By this time, though, with the Sioux Uprising underway, events had taken a dramatic turn on the Red River Trail and Pierre Bottineau, though he didn't know it yet, would be needed there.

Chapter Sixteen

Let Them Eat Grass

W hen Pierre Bottineau left the Fisk Expedition at Fort Union in early August 1862, there was no way to know that a Sioux uprising was about to begin on the trail he had just followed west. There's no record of the path Bottineau took as he made his way back to the Red River that August, but in all likelihood he followed a more or less direct path east, traveling near the Canadian border toward Pembina and Red River, where he could visit friends and relatives. Bottineau had also agreed to meet with government officials and Ojibwa chiefs later that month at the Grand Forks of the Red and Red Lake rivers, 70 miles south of Pembina. His plans were to act as a government interpreter again in treaty negotiations with the Ojibwa.

By this time, Bottineau had worked for years with government representatives dealing with the Natives. He probably began his career as guide and interpreter with the army sometime in the late 1840s, after initially taking similar jobs in the fur trade, although no records have been found to substantiate it. He served as an interpreter and guide for the American government in 1851, during the first treaty negations with the Ojibwa at Pembina, as well as other negotiations afterward. He had also taken part in a military policing activity with the American Army, tracking down an Ojibwa wanted for murder at Mille Lacs over the winter of 1854–55. Several times he took on the role as a guide for soldiers, mapping out possible locations for military forts in the West, including the establishment of the site at Fort Abercrombie where, unknown to Bottineau in the late summer of 1862, soldiers were about to find themselves surrounded and under siege by warring Sioux.

The first leg of Bottineau's ride east from Fort Union that August was uneventful. It was only after he reached Pembina on his way to Red River that he found himself involved in the war taking place on the trail 200 miles to the south. He stayed involved with that war, working as a scout and guide for General Henry Hastings Sibley, until the last of the skirmishes ended in Dakota Territory the following year.

Bottineau was half Ojibwa, traditional enemies of the Sioux, though it was said that his grandfather had actually been a Sioux captive in his mother's band. Any blood links to the tribe, however, had long before been discounted. The American writer Charles Carleton Coffin wrote that there was probably no man living at the time with more enemies than Bottineau, because any member of the Sioux nation would probably try to kill him on sight. Coffin's remarks were undoubtedly part of the hyperbole used by authors of the time writing for eastern audiences. Bottineau spoke the Dakota language, and he traded regularly with members of the tribe while he lived at St. Anthony. Still, there's little doubt occasional animosity flared between Bottineau and members of the Dakota tribes while he traveled the trails between Manitoba and St. Paul.

Coffin wrote that Bottineau had killed six Sioux warriors over the course of his life on the plains, as well as surviving several other narrow escapes. "To hear him tell of his adventures makes your hair stand on end," Coffin wrote. "If a Sioux buffalo hunter comes across this guide, there will be quick shooting on both sides, and ten to one the Indian will go down, for Bottineau is keen sighted, has a steady hand and is quick to act."

As Bottineau rode south toward Fort Abercrombie, he would not have known he would be busy in the aftermath of the Sioux war for several years to come, guiding soldiers to establish and build forts at Devils Lake, Pembina and other places as the government attempted to protect the frontier from further uprisings.

The next summer, in 1863, Bottineau led Alexander Ramsey and treaty commissioners to the Old Crossing on the Red Lake River, where he took on the job as an interpreter, once again in negotiations with the Ojibwa. This treaty, made soon after the Sioux hostilities came to an end, turned over almost the entire Red River Valley, with its long-used trail, to the United States government. By this time, however, with 10 more years of experience dealing with American authorities, the Natives were less willing to give up their land as easily as before.

Ramsey offered them twice as much per year as they had agreed to in 1851 during the first round of treaty negotiations for the right to passage along the trail. But that treaty had been rejected by the United States Senate, and in 1863, the new offer failed to satisfy the chiefs as the second round of negotiations got started. Little Rock, one of the Ojibwa spokesmen, told Ramsey, "If you had wanted a right of way over the roads and rivers, you should have consulted us before you took it."

It looked for a time as if no agreement would be made. At one point, Little Rock said he was going to withdraw from negotiations, through fear that "one who talks my own language is the weapon you are going to use against us." In this, he may have been speaking of Bottineau who, of course, was the interpreter. More telling, perhaps, Ramsey then asked Bottineau to speak with the chiefs on his own, which he did. Bottineau and his brother, Charles, who was a prominent trader at Pembina and was also there to assist in the negotiations, met with the chiefs along with a couple of other Métis and talked late into the night without representatives from the government present. In the morning, all but one of the chiefs, Matwakonoonind, agreed to a treaty that turned over nearly 10 million acres of land to the American government.

In exchange, the Natives were promised $20,000 per year for 20 years. The government earmarked $5000 of the total to be used for agricultural training and general education. There were other provisions as well, most notably one for the government to set aside $100,000 to be paid to the traders, including the Hudson's Bay Company, for losses they had supposedly incurred in their dealings with the Ojibwa. Despite the increased compensation, the treaty was a bitter pill for most of the chiefs to swallow. "When the master of life put you here he never told you that you should own the soil," said one of them.

Bottineau must have experienced some conflicting emotions as he persuaded the chiefs to accept the treaty.

He was, after all, half Ojibwa. His aging mother, still living in his home at Bottineau Prairie, was a member of the tribe. Many of his children would later enroll as tribe members. The day before the treaty was signed, one of the chiefs had balked at the agreement because, if he were to sign, he told Ramsey, "You forget that the land will be yours for as long as the world lasts." But that evening, Bottineau convinced most of the chiefs to change their minds, and the agreement they signed essentially completed the process of taking the bulk of the Red River Valley from the Native people of Minnesota and Dakota Territory. Years later, one of Bottineau's granddaughters told stories about the Ojibwa who used to come to visit Bottineau, and how some of them were still angry with him because he had helped the government when it took the Red River Trail and the land around it.

It should also be noted that one of the provisions and a later amendment in the 1863 treaty provided for 160 acres of land to be given to "each male adult half-breed who adopts the customs of civilized life or became a citizen of the United States and homesteads the claim for five years." The crude provision at least acknowledged there was a legitimate Métis claim to land the Red River Trail passed through, and it eventually tried to address the problem with a process similar to the method that would later be put in place in Manitoba, creating land "scrip" that Métis families could exchange for homesteads.

Treaty making started much earlier in Minnesota than it did in Manitoba, and the Pembina treaty was merely an extension of what had been happening for years. Lieutenant Zebulon Pike negotiated the first treaty with the Sioux in 1805, when he obtained a site for the American government that eventually became the Fort Snelling military base. Then, a long pause in treaty negotiations took place, until 1837 when treaties with the Ojibwa and Sioux gave Americans access to land on the east side of the Mississippi River. After that deal, no other major land transfers took place until after Minnesota became a territory in 1849.

However, Native land did not go unused by whites. Traders, usually with cooperation from the Natives, built posts throughout the region for nearly a century before any treaties came to Minnesota, and the first Protestant missionaries worked on Native land in the future state at least as early as the 1820s. On the Red River Trail, traders, drovers and emigrants crossed Native territory from the route's earliest days and usually went unmolested.

Soldiers, explorers, farmers going south to buy seed and all sorts of other folks began using the Red River Trail in the 1820s, coming in canoes, carts, on foot and horseback. Almost all arrived without permission or invitation. Few were particularly welcome, so it should have been no surprise that fighting flared up occasionally.

Charles Hess, a French Canadian trader, barely escaped death on the trail in 1822 after a Sioux raid. One of his two half-Ojibwa daughters and two other settlers from Red River with him were killed. Hess' group had been on the trail only a few days when, about 50 miles south of Pembina, a band of Dakota ambushed them. Just before the fighting started, Hess had gone off looking for a runaway horse; then, on coming across two buffalo on the prairie not far from the trail, he had ridden off to kill them. While he was away, the attack came. When he returned from the hunt, Hess discovered his two companions scalped and shot full of arrows. One of his daughters was dead, a knife left protruding from her chest. His other daughter was nowhere to be found.

Hess rode for help at Pembina, but the few people there at the time were afraid of another Sioux attack. Nobody would go back with him to bury his friends and daughter. On his own, Hess learned that a band of Yankton Sioux had abducted his surviving daughter and taken her to one of their hunting camps. As he rode into the village, several men stopped Hess; one stepped forward with bow and arrow in hand and asked him if he came as a friend or an enemy.

"You know me as your foe," Hess replied. "You know you have killed one of my daughters, and you have taken the other prisoner."

The Sioux stepped backwards and raised his bow, pointing an arrow at Hess' face. Within an instant, Hess pulled up his musket to defend himself. The Sioux quickly let his bow drop rather than chance getting shot. At that point, the other Natives came forward, praising Hess for his bravery and inviting him to feast with them. During the course of the meal, Hess was allowed to see his daughter, who said she had been well treated by her kidnappers.

Afterward, Hess tried to bribe the girl's abductor, but the Sioux refused to release her. Some neighboring Natives, friendly to Hess, arrived and tried to buy the girl for him, but the kidnapper still refused. Hess offered him two horses, and then four, but each proposed trade was rejected. Finally, Hess agreed to pay two white blankets, a chief's coat, a tin kettle, four guns, some powder, 200 bullets, a large quantity of blue beads and several yards of cloth for his daughter. Hess was unable to provide the goods immediately, so he had to leave his daughter in the camp for several days until he was able to get what he needed, on credit, from other traders. But a deal had been struck, and his daughter was eventually returned to him.

In 1823, a Scottish blacksmith named David Tully and his family were moving south from Red River. Near the present city of Grand Forks, not far from where Hess had his run-in with the Sioux, another band of the same tribe attacked the group, killing Tully and his wife, scalping one of his sons alive and abducting another.

The worry that accompanied those on the Red River Trail in the 1820s can also be seen in accounts taken from the diary of John Corcoran, an Irish settler at Red River who journeyed to St. Louis the summer after Tully was killed. Corcoran followed the trail with 200 others, but even in such large numbers they constantly feared ambush by the Sioux, though no attack came during the trip.

When Corcoran's party camped at Turtle River, a few days south of the colony, Corcoran wrote that the guides suspected Indians were in the vicinity because they saw no wild animals except for a single wolf. Instead of going to bed, Corcoran said, he and his companions "loaded our guns, filled our powder horns, furnished our shot pouches with ball, kindled a large fire, [and] sat up all night. [But] no danger appeared."

Right up until Minnesota statehood, the most common Native battles in the region were fought between the Sioux and Ojibwa. Violence between these traditional enemies could come anywhere, sometimes even at Red River, itself, or on the streets of early St. Paul. Tensions between the tribes were always on edge and easily transferred to relatives of the Ojibwa who, like Bottineau, were Métis. Cart drivers on the Red River Trail kept their weapons handy. Violence of one form or another could break out anywhere on the route, and it did, almost yearly. Sioux warriors ambushed and killed a dozen Métis on the trail in 1822 alone.

The violence seemed to grow worse as time went on, and the buffalo became harder to hunt. In the late 1830s, the most popular branch of the Red River Trail had already shifted from the Minnesota Valley to the Sauk River, partly because there were fewer chances to run into Sioux war parties on the new trail. Especially after the American Fur Company post at Lake Traverse was attacked, with the Sioux killing one of the clerks and seriously wounding another, most people avoided the southern trail whenever possible.

By 1844, tensions between Sioux and Métis had reached a point of near open warfare, which led to the construction of the Woods Trail farther north, away from the Sioux. Before the new branch of the trail was built, the Sioux had stopped traffic everywhere on the old branches of the trail between Manitoba and St. Paul. And despite a particular quarrel with the Métis, they directed their outrage at just about anyone who came along. One group of Missouri drovers, somewhat lost after driving their cattle across the Minnesota River on their way to Fort Snelling, ran into a Sioux war party northwest of present-day New Ulm.

The Sioux probably first assumed the men were from Red River. They surrounded them and demanded their guns. One of the drovers resisted and was killed. The three other men gave up immediately and were taken prisoner, stripped of their clothes and valuables, and marched to the Sioux camp. Two were tortured and killed, but one man escaped. He was found, naked and near death, a few days later by people from the village of the Sioux chief Sleepy Eyes. The man was cared for until he was strong enough to get to Fort Snelling and then return to Missouri.

Most of the violence directed against whites on the Red River Trail came at the hands of the Sioux, though not all of it. The Ojibwa avoided such trouble, but they were sometimes disgruntled with the situations they found themselves in and often resented the free use of their country by others. One Hudson's Bay Company employee following the Woods route in 1847 was stopped a few miles south of the international boundary by a band of unhappy Ojibwa. The Hudson's Bay man was bringing trade goods north, and the Ojibwa wanted to buy a few items, including some whiskey. When the HBC employee told the Natives it was against the law for the company to trade in the United States, the Ojibwa turned sour and took what they wanted anyway. At least this was the story the trader told to explain his missing whiskey.

One of James Sinclair's daughters, years after the fact, recounted how the party she was with in 1850 on the Woods branch of the Red River Trail went for several days without lighting a campfire because they were afraid the smoke might catch the attention of the Pillager band of Ojibwa. Others, too, spoke of depredations made by Pillagers along the Woods branch of the trail, which was, ironically, built and used in large part to avoid trouble with the Sioux.

Unlike the trail through Crow Wing, much of the Red River Trail that started on the west side of the Red River crossed land claimed by the Sioux for most of the distance between Red River and St. Paul, and it was the Sioux who the travelers feared most. Sioux territory encompassed the head-waters of the Red River and land west of that river as far north as the international boundary. Even north of the border, Sioux bands roamed the plains at will, following the buffalo. Occasionally, the Sioux camped on the edge of the Red River settlement, itself, despite the risk of open conflict with Ojibwa there. In addition to the troubles of 1844, open battles between the Sioux and Métis occurred in 1845, 1848, 1851, 1852 and 1855.

One of the largest Native battles ever fought in North America took place in the mid-1850s, west of the trail near today's Pilot Mound, Manitoba. Details of the fighting have been lost, but Métis buffalo hunters apparently came across a large band of Sioux near a ceremonial mound known as the "little dancing hill." It's unknown how many of the Métis were killed, but as many as 600 of the Sioux—some of them, perhaps, women and children—reportedly died.

Only two or three of the Sioux were allowed to live, the Métis said, so they could take the story of the battle back to their people as a warning. A couple of years earlier, a band of less than 100 Métis had successfully fought off another much larger force of 2000 Sioux farther south on the Grand Coteau of the Missouri, in present-day North Dakota. None of the Métis were killed in that fight, while an estimated 80 Sioux lost their lives.

In 1852, a few miles south of the international boundary in North Dakota, another incident involving the Sioux occurred near the trail, not far from today's Walhalla, North Dakota. A young missionary, who had arrived in the area earlier that year, was hard at work building his first cabin when several Sioux, passing through the area, evidently objected to a missionary working in the region. The Natives ambushed the man, shooting him with arrows from behind. Only a few years earlier, a new missionary on the trail at Traverse de Sioux had asked a pioneer Minnesota clergyman if he should first ask the Sioux for permission to build his planned mission. The older missionary shook his head and replied, "Not if you intend to stay."

Politicians started talking about treaties to obtain the last of the Sioux lands in Minnesota as soon as the territorial years began. In 1851, the Sioux gave up title to virtually all of southern and central Minnesota as far west as the Red River. They had negotiated to keep a strip of land along the upper Minnesota River as far west as Lake Traverse, but Congress unilaterally changed the terms of the treaty. No land was designated for the Sioux in the revised document, though a future grant was stipulated to be determined by the American president. Even with this drastic change, traders and politicians pressured the Sioux chiefs to go ahead with the land transfer, and the Dakota later received two small reservations in the long valley they had once owned.

In 1854 and 1855, in treaty negotiations where Pierre Bottineau acted as interpreter, the Ojibwa, too, were forced to sign treaties giving up large areas of their land. The first treaty took northeastern Minnesota from the Ojibwa. In the second treaty, the Natives gave up land south of Red Lake from the Rainy River to the Red. After this treaty, the Ojibwa essentially retained only the area of land east of the Big Fork River in northeastern Minnesota and the Red River Valley in the extreme northwest. This land included a long stretch of the Red River Trail south of Pembina on both sides of the river. Pierre Bottineau, of course, helped persuade the Ojibwa to give up most of this land, too.

Even so, the Ojibwa were probably more fortunate than the Sioux. They had been dealing with white traders and governments longer and were, consequently, more wary when treaty negotiations came along. And, in Minnesota, most lived farther north where, for at least one additional generation, there would be less pressure on them from the spreading white settlements creeping up the trail in the Red River Valley.

It was different for the Sioux. Settlers began moving onto Dakota land almost as soon as the 1851 treaty was signed at Traverse de Sioux. Whites started taking up claims before Congress approved the treaty; in fact, they started taking Dakota land three years before it would have been legal to do so under the terms set forth in the treaty. In these cases, settlers moved onto the land and then burned the bark homes and other property of the Dakota who had every legal right to be there.

In the Minnesota River Valley, there was nowhere left for the Dakota to live their traditional life. Some tried to adapt to the ways of the whites, attending the missionary churches and taking up farming at the two agencies established along the Minnesota River. Most of the tribe, though, lived largely off the once-a-year treaty payments and the credit they obtained from agency traders during the rest of the year. In 1862, when the government payment due in June failed to arrive, the traders refused to grant the Natives additional credit until the previous year's bills were paid. The Dakota, of course, were not able to pay those bills without the government payments they were owed.

By August, the treaty money still hadn't arrived, so some of the Sioux gathered at the Upper Agency and angrily demanded food from the storehouses to keep them from starving until the annuity payments came. Faced with the threat of a revolt, Indian Agent Thomas Galbraith convinced traders to issue a small amount of pork and flour. The Sioux took the offering grudgingly, knowing it was far less than they were entitled.

Downstream, at the mouth of the Redwood, traders at the Lower Agency still refused to give the Sioux anything until the annuity payment arrived from Washington. When Little Crow, probably the Dakota's most respected chief, gathered with others to demand the same provisions already obtained by fellow Sioux upriver, Galbraith agreed, but the traders balked. When the agent pressed them to give the Natives food, they turned to trader Andrew Myrick to ask what he thought.

"Let them eat grass," Myrick said, and the Sioux were given no food.

Little Crow had counseled his followers to take up the ways of the whites, but after he heard a trader say the Natives could "eat grass" if they were hungry, Little Crow agreed to lead his people in the Sioux Uprising of 1862.

Two days later, the Sioux Uprising began on a Sunday morning, August 17, when a few young Sioux killed four homesteaders in an apparently spontaneous assault. But other Dakota had already been talking of war. The time for action appeared to have arrived. Soon the Sioux were attacking and killing white settlers across the valley, north as far as the main route of the Red River Trail and west as far as the Red River

Valley. In a matter of weeks, more settlers had been killed than in any other Native conflict in the history of the United States.

For years, Little Crow had advocated that the Sioux take up the ways of the whites. The old ways had passed, he said. He lived in a frame house and attended the missionary church, but he had also been there to hear Myrick say the Natives could eat grass. When angry Sioux warriors came to him for leadership on the Sunday evening after the first settlers had been killed, Little Crow reluctantly agreed to go to war with them.

The previous year, at the council held at the agency for the treaty payment, Little Crow had complained about the way promises to his people had been broken. A famous visitor that year, Henry David Thoreau, wrote in a letter that Little Crow was the most prominent chief of the Sioux and that the Indians, having the advantage in point of truth and earnestness, gave the most eloquent speeches. They were, Thoreau said, "dissatisfied with the white man's treatment of them, and probably have reason to be."

On the morning of August 18, 1862, Little Crow led his warriors against the traders at the Redwood agency. The fighting started at Myrick's store, where two clerks were killed. While the violence was taking place downstairs, Myrick crawled out of a second-floor window to escape, but he was shot as he jumped to the ground behind the building. Within minutes, nine others at the agency were dead. When the bodies were found, Andrew Myrick's mouth had been stuffed with grass.

But the Sioux Uprising in Minnesota was not over. Little Crow and his followers fell on settlers wherever they found them. Many were killed on the road, trying to escape to New Ulm or some other refuge. Dozens of women and children were taken hostage, though it was more typical for them to be killed outright along with the men. When word of the attacks reached Fort Ridgely, on the first day of the uprising, a party of 46 soldiers rode toward the Lower Agency. By evening, only 20 of them were alive to struggle back to the fort. Meanwhile, the attacks had spread to the Upper Agency, and small groups of roving Sioux spread fear throughout Minnesota all the way north to the Red River settlement.

In the midst of the killing, there were Sioux who heroically hid white or mixed-blood friends or led them to safety. Slowly, white resistance mounted. When Fort Ridgely was under siege, 200 soldiers and the citizens taking refuge there repelled 800 Sioux warriors in the course of three attacks spread over as many days. At New Ulm, after the Sioux failed to take Fort Ridgely, nearly 200 buildings were burned to the ground, but in the end, the town's defenders turned back the Sioux. At St. Peter, Henry Hastings Sibley, the old fur trader turned politician and now Army officer, began preparing a mostly volunteer army to go after Little Crow and his warriors.

Meanwhile, with the failures at Fort Ridgely and New Ulm, Sioux resolve began to dissipate. Little Crow led a wagon train of his people and a number of hostages upriver, where he was able to strike at settlers farther north and also, he hoped, get other Sioux bands farther west more involved in the fighting.

When Sibley followed, the Sioux bungled a surprise attack on the soldiers camped at Wood Lake, near the Upper Agency. Once more, Little Crow fled northwest along the old Red River Trail, but now, at the end of September, only some of his people continued with him. The rest waited in their camp, along with 269 hostages, where they surrendered to Sibley four days later.

Defeat was already facing Little Crow's people, but the fighting was still not over. When violence broke out in the Minnesota Valley, many of the Sioux living farther west joined in, terrorizing people on the trail between St. Cloud and Breckenridge. A stagecoach was captured and the driver killed. Settlers at Breckenridge were attacked. Six men were killed at a trading post on Lake Traverse. People fled to Fort Abercrombie, but the Sioux surrounded the post and kept it under siege for a month.

In the midst of the troubles with the Sioux, Pierre Bottineau showed up at the end of August, after riding south from Pembina with Rolette and the other volunteers. Bottineau first arrived at Georgetown with the others and set to work helping settlers who were cut off from Fort Abercrombie by the Sioux during the height of the uprising. Along with the settlers, Norman Kittson had been caught at Georgetown when the violence started, and he had a year's supply of goods belonging to the Hudson's Bay Company he wanted to move north. By the time Bottineau and help from Pembina arrived, the settlers had already decided on an overland escape up the Red River Trail, while Kittson tried to slip downriver by steamboat.

Packing the year's entire supply of trade goods on the *International*, Kittson left in the middle of the night. Instead of making an escape, however, the overloaded steamboat ran aground, and Kittson had to transfer his cargo to wagons and join the settlers going north on the trail. According to one story, the second night out, with the settlers corralled in a camp near where Kittson had abandoned the *International*, the group heard a blood-chilling Indian war whoop in the darkness. Most were terrified, but when men went to investigate, it turned out to be Bottineau having a little fun with them after drinking some of the whiskey Kittson had missed when he unloaded the *International*.

On their way up the Red River Trail toward Manitoba, near present-day Grand Forks, Bottineau and the others were held up, not by Sioux, but by angry Ojibwa. For several weeks, Natives from across the valley had been waiting at the Grand Forks of the Red and Red Lake rivers for the promised appearance of American treaty commissioners. The commissioners had dropped their plans to attend the council as soon as the Sioux uprising began but didn't bother to send word of their decision to the Ojibwa.

By the time Bottineau showed up, without the treaty commissioners, the Ojibwa had lost patience. Some were hungry. All of them were angry. Over Kittson's strenuous but unenforceable objections, the Ojibwa helped themselves to thousands of dollars worth of Hudson's Bay Company freight. In another year, the Ojibwa would be charged handsomely for what they took, but for the time being, Kittson and the company he now represented were out of luck.

Bottineau apparently went no farther north with the settlers before returning, briefly, to besieged Fort Abercrombie, where he slipped through the Sioux lines to take word of the army's plight to Sauk Center, where he could get reinforcements for the fort. Once help finally arrived late in September, the Sioux departed, and the siege at Fort Abercrombie came to an end.

Sibley wound up the fighting in western Minnesota that fall after many of the Sioux gave up. The Sioux who remained free either fled farther west to escape into Dakota Territory or headed north to the Red River settlement, where they found protection from American troops by crossing the international boundary. By the following year, while Sibley and Bottineau pursued the Sioux in a somewhat frustrating chase through Dakota Territory as far west as the Missouri River, Major Edwin A.C. Hatch came north on the Red River Trail to Pembina to patrol the border area. He brought three cavalry companies he had put together at Fort Snelling, along with a fourth company, known as the Mounted Rangers, that was composed almost entirely of Métis from Red River.

It is noteworthy that while American forces were able to put together a company of mounted rangers from the settlement in a relatively short time, Red River itself failed to raise its own militia. The people had petitioned for one to protect themselves, but the Hudson's Bay Company stood in the way, silently opposed to organizing the Métis people of the region in any force that might, it was feared, one day be used to take away its power. Despite the danger, the company was more afraid of losing control of their territory to the Métis than they were of the Sioux.

With no opposition from local forces, by early 1863, at least 500 destitute Sioux, much to the dismay of the Hudson's

Bay Company and the residents of Red River, were living north
of the border, and more were coming all the time. Still others,
including Little Crow's dwindling band, came and went from
Manitoba as they saw fit. The new governor of Rupert's Land,
Alexander Dallas, tried to negotiate with the Sioux, but without a militia, he had no real power to make them leave, nor
could he do anything else of consequence.

The Sioux brought medals and other items that had
been given to them when they had joined the British in the
fight against the Americans in the War of 1812. They had been
promised help, they said, if the Americans ever caused them
trouble. Now they wanted to collect on that promise. At Red
River, though, they got no help from the British.

Eventually, Dallas offered the Sioux food and ammunition if they would give their word to use the ammunition
only for hunting and promised to leave the settlement immediately. The Sioux took what they were given and, true to their
word, left Red River. But instead of going back to the United
States, they moved only a few miles west, just beyond the Métis
settlement at White Horse Plains. The Sioux were well north of
the American border, but they were still too close to Red River
for the comfort of the people of the settlement.

The international boundary had become a nuisance for
residents on both sides of the border. The Americans wanted to
capture the Sioux at Red River, particularly two chiefs, Shakopee and Medicine Bottle, who probably more than any of the
others in Manitoba had helped instigate the violence. The army,
though, was thwarted by the international boundary.

Governor Dallas and the settlers at Red River wanted
to get rid of the Sioux, but the settlers didn't have a militia to

do it, and Dallas was afraid to create one because it would give the Métis more power. At one point, Dallas invited Major Hatch to cross the border and capture the Sioux with some of his soldiers, but Hatch had no official authorization to go after the Sioux in British territory, so he declined.

In the meantime, several residents at Red River, led by A.G. Bannatyne, took matters into their own hands. A few of the men befriended the two chiefs, plied them with liquor, drugged them with the opiate laudanum and then kidnapped them, taking them down the trail to Hatch at Pembina. The major took the two chiefs south to be hanged. Shakopee and Medicine Bottle, by escaping up the trail to Canada, had avoided the execution that had already come to most of the Sioux leadership. But their time had arrived, and they, too, would be hanged at Fort Snelling in 1865.

In 1864, after the Sioux war had essentially ended in the United States, about 3500 Minnesota Sioux were still living near Red River or farther west on the Canadian prairie. Two years later, another 2000 arrived, coming out of hiding on the American plains. Some eventually returned to the United States, but for six years, the Sioux in Manitoba and Saskatchewan led a precarious and troublesome existence. Only after Canada took control of the British Northwest from the Hudson's Bay Company did at least some of the Sioux sign treaties, along with other Native people in western Canada. For these Sioux, signing the treaty finally put the consequences of the Minnesota uprising behind them.

The Sioux of Manitoba, despite their initial difficulties, came out of the uprising in somewhat better shape than many of those who remained south of the border. Pierre Bottineau took on the job of guide and scout for General Henry Sibley in 1863 as he moved through Dakota Territory trying to chase down the remaining Sioux who had participated in the uprising. In the end, the army pushed most of the Sioux into a marginal existence farther west on the plains or scared them over the border into Manitoba. A newspaper correspondent covering the chase wrote that Pierre Bottineau "is the guide of the expedition and if there is rock, hill, creek, ford or clump of bushes on the whole territory of Dakota that he is not acquainted with I should like to hear of it. He has led us with a perfect eye for over 800 miles and is still at the head guiding us over these trackless plains with unerring certainty."

Little Crow, returning to Minnesota after a stay in Manitoba, was shot and killed in July 1863 by a farmer and his son back in the original Dakota homeland. The old chief had been spotted picking berries near the town of Hutchinson. After he was shot, someone there scalped him and put his body on display in the middle of town.

Almost all of Little Crow's followers had abandoned him by then. Banished from the Minnesota River Valley, most of the unfortunate Sioux who remained alive were moved to reservations farther west. Little Crow's ignoble death was probably better than that of the 39 Sioux leaders hanged at Mankato, Minnesota, near the great bend of the Minnesota River in late December 1862, in the largest mass execution in American history.

Originally, 307 Sioux were sentenced to death, but President Lincoln, at the urging of the Minnesota Episcopal

Bishop, Henry Whipple, reduced the sentences for 268 of the condemned. Two years later, the Sioux chiefs Shakopee and Medicine Bottle were captured and sent down the trail from Red River to be hanged at Fort Snelling, bringing the total number of Dakota executions to 41.

Meanwhile, more than 500 settlers had been killed in the uprising, which was also called the Minnesota Massacre. Many others had been wounded, raped, kidnapped and terrorized. More than 40,000 people fled their homes, many never to return. It's impossible to know exactly how many people, white and Native, died in the Sioux uprising and its aftermath, but it's apparent that more settlers lost their lives than in any other Native confrontation on the North American continent.

The last report of a death related to the uprising didn't come until 1919, when a Minnesota man cutting wood found a mummified body wedged inside a hollow maple tree. The body was that of a former settler named Jean La Rue, who had escaped to the woods as Sioux warriors approached his cabin in the midst of the uprising.

La Rue apparently climbed into the tree to hide and then slipped too far into the crevice. Along with the body, the woodcutter found $783.50 in cash, a rifle, bullet pouch and powder horn, along with a journal in which La Rue had written, in an entry dated August 29, 1862, "Can not get out; surely must die. If ever found send me and all my money to my mother, Suzanne La Rue, near Tarascon, in the province of Bouches Du Phone, France."

The mother, of course, had died many years before. Authorities failed to find any other relatives.

Chapter Seventeen

A New Province

L ong after the Sioux Uprising of 1862 and the war that followed had run their course, an apocryphal story circulated about the execution of Medicine Bottle and Shakopee. It was said that, just as the noose was placed around Shakopee's neck, he heard a train whistle in the distance. Supposedly, he listened to the sound and then said, "As the white man comes in, the Indian goes out."

It's a poignant story but somewhat unlikely to have happened. Railroads moved steadily west toward Minnesota until the middle of the 1850s, when construction suddenly stalled near the Mississippi River. Nothing of much consequence happened with railroad building in Minnesota for years afterward. Even by the end of the Civil War in 1865, when Shakopee and Medicine Bottle were hanged, train tracks had barely entered the state.

There had been the usual railroad promotional schemes in Minnesota before the war, but not one rail was laid inside the state's borders until 1861, when the Minnesota and Pacific Railroad put down a miniscule half mile of track. The next year the railroad managed to lay another 10 miles of road between St. Paul and St. Anthony, but when Shakopee was hanged at Fort Snelling, there were barely 50 miles of track in the entire state. Shakopee might have died without ever seeing

a railroad train, and in all probability he went to the gallows
without hearing the lonesome wail of a steam whistle on that
early Minnesota morning.

The Civil War had diverted resources away from Minnesota, just as the Panic of 1857 had stalled the state's economy
a few years earlier. And during the war, the Sioux Uprising
frightened many of the homesteaders away. Once the Civil
War ended, however, the economy changed in a hurry. Settlers
streamed into Minnesota again. New homesteaders took up
land in the southern and central parts of the state first, and
then they spread farther west, moving steadily toward the Red
River. Railroad construction got underway in earnest.

By the late 1860s, life at Selkirk's old colony was finally
showing signs of relatively rapid change, too. For the people of
the British Northwest, events in Minnesota and distant Canada had finally sparked hope for a new day. The economic
boom in Minnesota after the Civil War inevitably spilled
north with the waters of the Red. Several St. Paul merchants,
trying to get a jump on the Red River trade, moved north to set
up shop in Winnipeg.

Everyone knew that the Hudson's Bay Company would
soon be forced to give up control of Rupert's Land. More than
ever, merchants in St. Paul began to look at the region north of
the border, at the other end of the Red River Trail, as an inevitable and permanent extension of their local economy. For the
first time, perhaps, merchants in St. Paul began to see the trail
as a transportation link that actually went somewhere, instead
of just a trail from an obscure settlement in the wilderness that
brought them furs and hides.

Outside of Minnesota, however, people in the United States had little interest in trade with Red River. British links with the Confederacy during the Civil War provoked widespread anti-British sentiment outside the South, and when a reciprocity trade agreement with the eastern Canadian colonies came up for renewal in 1866, the United States, despite opposing sentiments in Minnesota and other border states, let the treaty lapse. As far as most Americans were concerned, if Canada wanted trade with the United States, it could join the union. Annexation was possible, reciprocal trade in any other form unlikely.

Annexation, not surprisingly, had considerably less appeal in Canada than in the United States, unless the annexation under discussion was for Canada, itself, to annex Red River and the British Northwest. Talk of reviving the old North West Company trade route from Canada to Rupert's Land with a combination of Great Lakes steamships and new roads to Red River (thereby stealing the Red River trade from Minnesota) circulated in Toronto as early as the 1850s. The undertaking was wildly unrealistic, but it was attempted. And while the notion of a viable Great Lakes route to Red River failed, the dream of creating a Canadian nation reaching from the Atlantic to the Pacific took root. In Ontario, the notion was prevalent at least a decade before a confederation of the eastern Canadian provinces took place in 1867.

Scattered immigrants from Ontario began showing up at Red River in the late 1850s, and they harbored distinctly Canadian versions of Manifest Destiny. But to most of the residents of Red River, who had hardly any more connection to Canada than they did to the United States, the Canadian nationalists appeared to be of questionable character, especially to the Métis. In October 1859, William Coldwell and William Buckingham, two newspapermen from Ontario, came up the Crow Wing branch of the Red River Trail on the east side of the river with three ox-carts carrying a printing press, paper and ink they had purchased in St. Paul.

The *Nor'Wester*, the paper they started at Red River, became the first newspaper published in all of what was to become western Canada. For the next decade, the *Nor'Wester* changed hands and took on new partners, but it consistently promoted a Canadian expansionist view that reflected the biases of its owners, with no apparent regard for the truth or consequences of the words it published. Accuracy was never as important as argument at the *Nor'Wester*, and, surprisingly, its inaccuracies often mirrored those in the St. Paul newspapers. Like the *Nor'Wester*, newspapers in Minnesota exaggerated support for American annexation of western Canada. The only difference was that the Manitoba newspaper's exaggerations were meant to provoke a bellicose reaction back in eastern Canada, whereas the Minnesota papers saw its arguments as prophesying and legitimizing what they hoped would be a positive outcome for Minnesota business interests.

The Canadian expansionists at Red River were small in number, but vocal, and for the most part, recent arrivals. The Métis saw the Canadians as bigoted and untrustworthy, and during the 1860s, Canadian partisans at Red River seemed to do what they could to live up to the poor assessment. Members of the Canadian party formed a short-lived

Republic of Manitobah, apparently to speed Canadian annexation. Others, advocating Canadian rule and championed by the *Nor'Wester*, found themselves in court and even jail, before breaking out and essentially undermining, for personal and partisan purposes, what little formal law there was in the region under the Hudson's Bay Company.

Sympathy for Canadian annexation was also weakened, in 1868, after grasshoppers destroyed crops at Red River and the summer buffalo hunt failed. Starvation appeared imminent for many at the settlement, and the outside world responded with aid. The St. Paul Chamber of Commerce donated $4000 to help the cause. The Minnesota Legislature passed a bill to send money. In London, the Hudson's Bay Company raised £4000 from private donations. The Province of Ontario promised $5000, although it never sent anything.

The new country of Canada offered only a make-work project, which turned out to further undermine any pro-Canada sentiment that might have existed in the general population at Red River. The plan was to pay workers $18 a month to build a road from Fort Garry to Lake of the Woods, a crucial step to connect Manitoba with Ontario through the Great Lakes. But when the government surveyors finally arrived in Red River, Canadian expansionists from Ontario were given most of the jobs. If the road building was meant to engender goodwill toward Canada among the general population—and in Red River that meant the Métis—it failed.

Meanwhile, in Minnesota in the late 1860s, with the chance for trade reciprocity with Canada and Red River lost, talk turned, seriously for the first time, from trade to outright annexation. The notion sprang more from the desire to preserve trade than the appeal of nationalism, or so-called Manifest Destiny. The general feeling seemed to be that no railroad could ever be built across northern Ontario, and without a railroad, the new country of Canada lacked the financial resources to create adequate economic ties to Manitoba and the British Northwest.

When the land transfer from the Hudson's Bay Company to Canada was announced in 1869, the *St. Paul Press* wrote: "... if politically it [Rupert's Land] belongs to Canada, geographically...it belongs not to Canada, but to Minnesota."

In the long run, however, the historical tide was receding for Minnesota. Only one last opportunity presented itself for keeping the commerce of the British Northwest moving over the old route of the Red River Trail. If political maneuverings were unable to bring about annexation, perhaps the people of Red River could be enticed to join the American union on their own. In 1869 and 1870, the Métis of Red River, with unintentional help from the Canadian government, made that idea seem at least possible, and for a brief moment, almost likely.

The year after Canada attempted its road-building project, the new dominion made a bigger blunder in its move toward annexation of the Red River Country. Before a deed for transferring Rupert's Land from the Hudson's Bay Company to Canada had been signed, Canada sent surveyors to Red River to lay out homesteads in a system based on the American model of land division, surveying 36 square 640-acre sections inside six-mile-square townships. No violation of existing property rights was intended, at least not at that time, but the whole thing looked suspicious to most folks at Red

River, where people lived on river lot homesteads using the French system of Quebec rather than the square, 160-acre quarter sections used in most of the rest of North America.

Moreover, the Métis realized that if they left matters to Ottawa, the likely outcome would be that the small Canadian party at Red River would be called on to run the show once Canada took over. When Canadian officials arrived from the east, the Métis and most other long-term residents figured

Louis Riel led the Métis in the Red River Resistance of 1869–70, actions that eventually allowed Manitoba to become part of Canada as a province equal to the others and with a list of civil rights guaranteed to its residents.

they would be pushed to the edges where their needs and views would not matter.

Under the leadership of Louis Riel, a charismatic, young, Montreal-educated idealist who would later appear to be of somewhat unstable mind, the Métis put a halt to the surveying. A few days later, they formed what they called a National Committee and enrolled several hundred men in a local militia. By this time, back in Ontario, William McDougall had been named the new Lieutenant Governor of Rupert's Land, although the land transfer had not yet officially taken place. No one at Red River had been asked if they wanted Canada to annex Rupert's Land, least of all the Métis. No one there had been consulted about anything, but McDougall was on his way up the Red River Trail, with a small entourage that included his family, several other Ontario immigrants and a number of wagons filled with rifles that McDougall meant to use to arm a new militia he intended to create once he arrived.

The trail was dry that October, easy going, with the weather, at first, sunny and warm. There were thousands of ducks and geese along the way, so some hunting was offered for diversion. A physician named John O'Donnell, who had only joined the caravan at St. Cloud because he was going the same direction, was told by the St. Paul businessman James J. Hill sometime earlier that McDougall would run into trouble if he went to Manitoba without first consulting the Métis. When O'Donnell relayed this information to McDougall, the latter said he had more reliable information and there was no cause for concern.

Before McDougall left St. Paul, a man on the street had handed him a letter and walked away. The letter probably contained a warning, but McDougall promptly threw it away without bothering to read it. After McDougall's caravan moved into the valley north of Fort Abercrombie, the nights turned colder. Now and again there were days with snow in the air, and along the trail, mounted Métis occasionally rode past, galloping hard from the south, going around McDougall and his wagons, on the trail north to Pembina. These Métis scouts let Louis Riel and the Métis of Red River know everything McDougall did long before he got anywhere near the Manitoba border.

A few miles south of Fort Garry, Riel barricaded the trail, and when McDougall reached Pembina, a courier gave him a message from the Métis leader instructing him to remain in American territory. When McDougall ignored the order and continued on to a Hudson's Bay Company post just north of the boundary, soldiers from Riel's army escorted the would-be Canadian Lieutenant Governor and his wagons of rifles back to the United States.

A few days later, while McDougall stewed at Pembina, the Métis seized Fort Garry. Riel sent word to the English-speaking residents of Red River that they could select delegates and join his National Committee in a convention to consider the future of the region. The English-speaking residents, who had their own reservations about Canadian rule, accepted the offer. Like the French-speaking Métis, most English-speaking people at Red River distrusted the Canadian partisans and worried about the rights of long-term residents if the Canadian government took control of the region. Also like the Métis, the English-speaking population of Red River, excluding the Canadian party, carried no particular loyalty to Canada. Few of them had ever been there, though most of

William McDougall came west to become the first lieutenant governor of Manitoba, but members of a Métis militia stopped him at the international border. He attempted to crush the Métis resistance, but things only became worse before he retreated to Ontario.

them probably saw some form of attachment to that young country as their best course for the future.

In retrospect, it is surprising how accommodating Riel, with 80 percent of the population Métis, appeared to be to the English-speaking minority. It's hard to imagine that, had the numbers been reversed, the English speakers would have extended the same courtesies. In fact, when the situation did reverse itself a few years later, after a boom in immigration from eastern Canada, the rights guaranteed the Métis at Confederation were wiped out.

When the two groups at Red River, French and English, came together in Riel's National Committee, however, they appeared united in the outcome they sought—the protection of the rights of existing residents—but in the following days of debate, they found no agreement on a means to reach that goal. When Riel suggested that a provisional government be set up, the English-speaking delegates balked. They said they would have to consult with the people they represented before making such an important decision. The convention adjourned for a week, until the first of December, to allow them to decide.

During intervening days, the idea arose in the English-speaking community that Red River's best course would be to reconstitute the old Council of Assiniboia, the quasi-governing body used under Hudson's Bay Company rule. Oscar Malmros, the American Counsel at Red River, urged Riel to support the compromise rather than take the more radical approach of forming an entirely new government. Riel would probably have followed that advice except that, in the meantime, McDougall undercut the Canadian position once more.

On November 29, just two days before the convention was to meet again, McDougall crossed the 49th parallel with a plan for the Canadian party at Red River to launch a counter revolution that would back him and, he hoped, draw other supporters from the English-speaking residents of Red River, leaving the majority of the population out of the equation. Additional support for McDougall, beyond the small group of Canadian partisans, was almost impossible to find at Red River, however, and his plan soon fizzled. But the attempt was enough to spark Riel into establishing a new provisional government in

Manitoba, without waiting to see what the English-speaking residents would do.

There were nearly 10,000 Métis at Red River, some of whom spoke English as a first language and were less likely to support the more radical ideas of their French-speaking brethren. Still, as the leader of the majority of the people at Red River, Riel went ahead with his new Métis government. In the end, he was willing to negotiate with the government of Canada for a union beneficial to the people of the region. But he needed to ensure that negotiations took place first, and he insisted that any plans Canada had for Red River had to be approved by the people who lived there before any union would be allowed to proceed.

When McDougall's disastrous foray into Manitoba was turned back, he retreated all the way down the Red River Trail to St. Paul, and then home to Canada. Behind him, he left several members of the Canadian party jailed at Fort Garry for their part in his aborted counter-revolution. On the surface, it looked as if the chances of American annexation had improved dramatically. Certainly, the Americans at Red River, who were almost as numerous as the Canadians, thought so. In reality, the United States could do little, short of outright war, to take Manitoba and the rest of Rupert's Land away from Canada. The likelihood is that Riel knew this fact and kept contacts open with his American friends simply as a backup plan, in case negotiations with the Canadians failed.

By January 1870, when Donald Smith, the new head of the Hudson's Bay Company, arrived in Manitoba as an envoy from the Canadian government, American influence had

James J. Hill (left), along with several Canadian Associates, built the first railroad to connect St. Paul with Winnipeg. Its tracks essentially replaced the Red River Trail in 1879.

become inconsequential. The primary purpose of Riel's provisional government had probably always been to work something out with the Canadian government that would protect the rights of Red River residents, French and English. Smith came to see what arrangements could be made to bring the old Hudson's Bay territory into the new Canadian confederation, and Riel was willing to work with him, drawing up a list of democratic rights necessary to be included in any agreement.

In March, another harbinger of Manitoba's future arrived at Red River, in the person of James Jerome Hill. Hill was a Canadian, but he hadn't come to join the Canadian party resident at Red River. He had come as a St. Paul businessman interested in the development of the Red River country and the British Northwest. Hill soon became involved in steamboat trade on the Red River. A few years later, he led a group of business associates, including Donald Smith and the old Pembina fur trader, Norman Kittson, in a spectacular takeover of the St. Paul and Pacific Railroad. And before the decade of the 1870s ended, Hill and his associates turned their railroad into the St. Paul, Minneapolis and Manitoba line that stretched from the Minnesota capital to Winnipeg, giving Minnesota the link it wanted to the Canadian West.

That first year, when Hill came to Red River, the community was in the midst of its revolution. It was a time before Manitoba's political future had been determined. Hill stayed only a short time, but he left convinced of the region's future wealth.

For his return trip from Winnipeg, Hill hired Pierre Bottineau, who was in the Red River settlement that spring. Bottineau had taken a group of Americans, organized by Nathanial Langford, north on the trail shortly after Hill arrived. What the Americans were doing at Red River at that particular time is somewhat clouded in history, though it's known that they met with Riel twice while they were there, which was certainly no accident. Afterward, Langford, a businessman, was in touch with James Wilkes Taylor, a leading proponent of economic and political ties between Minnesota and Manitoba, and J.J. Cook, who probably financed Langford's trip north as a scouting expedition for his Northern Pacific Railroad.

One account has Riel telling Langford that though he was personally in favor of American annexation, he thought the Métis did not particularly support it. There are only scattered references about Bottineau taking on the role of guide for Hill after getting Langford through to Red River that spring.

According to a tale Hill told about the trip, Bottineau had dislocated his arm trying to help push a Red River cart across a small stream. Hill had to sit on his guide and hold him down to reset the injured arm, and in the telling of the tale, he

John A. Macdonald was Canada's first prime minister, but he badly misjudged the Métis of Red River when his government annexed the territory of the HBC without consulting the people of Red River. When the Métis resisted, he quickly decided to negotiate Manitoba's entry into Canada instead.

displayed a prejudice toward the Métis that was common at that time. Hill, who had once intended to become a doctor, used a rope and a box-elder branch leveraged in the cartwheel to apply the needed force for the procedure. He said that by twisting the rope, the branch put steadily increasing pressure on Bottineau's shoulder, until, with his guide screaming in pain, the bone snapped into place.

About the time Hill and Bottineau left on the trail for Minnesota, word reached Red River that Canada's first prime minister, John A. Macdonald, had agreed, in principle, to the Métis demands for citizenship, as well as their list of specific civil rights, leaving only the details to be worked out later. Macdonald had apparently taken the people of Red River for granted in his negotiations to acquire the Hudson's Bay Company lands for Canada. Once the situation proved troublesome, he moved with some dispatch, selecting Smith to go west to negotiate for Canada. Smith, in turn, talked Riel into sending Manitoba representatives down the Red River Trail, and then east to Canada, to negotiate with the Canadian government directly.

The result was the Manitoba Act, which was introduced in the Canadian Parliament in May 1870 and became law in just 10 days. To ensure that everything went smoothly, and probably to make it apparent to the Americans that Canada was, indeed, assuming control, Macdonald also sent a troop of soldiers across the Great Lakes and northwestern Ontario, avoiding the Red River Trail to take an all-Canadian route to the new province of Manitoba. As the army marched from the banks of the Red to the gates of Fort Garry, Riel and his lieutenants slipped away to avoid arrest, escaping down the trail into the United States.

Chapter Eighteen
Red River by Rail

Louis Riel had a couple reasons to scoot quickly down the Red River Trail into Dakota Territory in the summer of 1870 after Canadian soldiers arrived at Fort Garry. For starters, some say he had been secretly given money to disappear into the United States, thus relieving the Canadian government of the controversy and trouble his apprehension might create. For his part, Riel escaped to avoid Canadian retribution, official or otherwise, for his role in the Red River Rebellion, especially his order to execute Thomas Scott, one of the Canadians at Red River who had joined McDougall in the armed resistance to Riel's government.

Riel left Manitoba on the Red River Trail and found refuge at Antoine Gingras' home and trading post just south of the international boundary. His efforts at Red River had, at a minimum, sped up the creation of a new Canadian province and made the Red River country part of Canada. And for a time, a short time, Riel's efforts demonstrated the strengths and desires of the Métis people.

The irony is that the result added to the political demise of the Métis. Partly by national design and partly by the inevitable explosion of the non-Métis population in the Canadian West after Manitoba became part of Canada, the welfare of the Métis, even the rights guaranteed them in the Manitoba Act, would soon be forgotten. They had demanded rights of citizenship sought by free people everywhere as the price of Manitoba's entry into the Canadian federation. But once the battle had been won, once the great fur company had been pushed aside and free trade and political change in the name of Canada came to the Northwest, the Métis, like their Aboriginal cousins, found themselves a minority in their own land.

Thomas Scott (above) was one of the men that William McDougall encouraged to stage an armed uprising against the Métis. But Scott, a rabid anti-Catholic from northern Ireland, was captured by Riel's forces, imprisoned at Fort Garry and shot for his role in the plot.

As immigrants poured into Manitoba, the last of the buffalo disappeared from the plains. The land that had been open and free was all too soon fenced and owned by people from other places. The Métis scrip that had promised homesteads instead of reservations would somehow fail. The Métis had long battled with the Hudson's Bay Company, but once the war was won, once political change came to the Northwest, it seemed that the interests of the old fur company and the traditional life of the Red River Métis were more dependent on each other than either had realized.

More than anything, it was a railroad that changed it all. Railroads and riverboats on the Red River had chipped away at the old trail for years, stealing passengers and freight, making larger and larger parts of the trail unnecessary. But the closer the railroads came to Manitoba, the more economical transportation costs became. When the St. Paul and Pacific railroad reached St. Cloud in 1866, the frontier settlement turned into an alternate trading point for the Red River carts. The fur trade was still centered in St. Paul, but St. Cloud became a shipping point for some of the Red River goods coming and going on the trail, almost the de facto southern end of the Red River Trail.

Steamboat traffic on the Red River also displaced part of the old Red River cart traffic, but the winding, slow-moving river, open only a few months in the best of years, was too undependable to replace the trail entirely. Steamboats and rivers, by themselves, could never handle the amount of trade that already passed between Manitoba and Minnesota. Steamboats and partially completed railroads altered the role of the old trail, but they did not immediately bring an end to the ox-cart route. That would have to wait.

When the Canadian government made Manitoba part of the new Dominion of Canada in 1870, Prime Minister John A. Macdonald had already been dreaming about a railroad to link eastern Canada with the Pacific. When British Columbia became a province the year after Manitoba joined, he turned his dream into a government promise.

Before a Canadian railroad could reach Manitoba, however, Bottineau's new friend, James J. Hill and a trio of Canadian or Canadian-born associates built an American line from St. Paul to Manitoba. The new steel tracks would essentially exchange the Red River Trail for a Minnesota railroad in the late 1870s. In addition, Hill and his associates ensured that Manitoba's economic connection to Minnesota would remain supreme for a few more years.

Hill first turned his attention to the potential riches of the Red River country after his 1870 visit to Manitoba, when he hired Pierre Bottineau as his guide for the trip back down the trail to St. Paul. Hill had come to the Minnesota capital in 1856, when he was just 18. He was a somewhat romantically inclined youth who left his home in Ontario to seek his fortune in the outside world. When he left the family farm, Hill imagined himself going to the Orient to find his fortune, but as things turned out, he would win more wealth than he ever dreamed after he built his railroad to Manitoba.

Hill took a simple job as a clerk in St. Paul, chronicling goods arriving and departing by steamboat on the Mississippi River. But Hill was a fast learner, an avid reader and ambitious from the beginning. He studied and learned about everything he came across, from engineering to history. Before long, he turned his job on the docks into a new business, as a shipping agent. From there, Hill took what he had learned of the St. Paul commodities market and started buying and selling coal. Within a few months, he had cornered the entire Minnesota coal market.

By 1870, when Hill scouted the Red River country with Pierre Bottineau, he was already one of the richest men in the state, and he became convinced that more wealth lay for the picking in the Red River Valley. After he returned from Manitoba that year, Hill set up a new transportation and trading company and, later that summer, the new firm began ferrying goods by flatboat down the Red River. By the following spring, Hill had a new steamboat, the *Selkirk*, working on the Red. This put him in direct competition with Norman Kittson, who now represented the Hudson's Bay Company in Minnesota and managed the company's steamboat business on the Red River.

By the following year, Hill and Kittson had joined forces. The Hudson's Bay Company had withdrawn from its silent partnership with Kittson after Hill complained to the American government, pointing out that his was the only truly American line on the river. Once Hill and Kittson amalgamated, their steamboats held a monopoly on the Red. They charged what they wanted but also encouraged freight and passenger service in ways that had never been done when Hudson's Bay Company interests controlled the business. Steamboat use was no longer geared to the particular needs of the HBC. The water route had disadvantages, notably a very short season, but for the first time, river traffic began to truly compete with trade on the cart trail.

But Hill's and Kittson's takeover of the steamboat business was only the beginning. The end of the trail would come after they put together a railroad—a railroad that would almost immediately reduce the colorful cart trains to memory. The railroad was all Hill's idea, but Kittson, along with the old Hudson's Bay trader Donald Smith and a Montreal banker named George Stephen, each played a role in what became one of the most spectacular business takeovers in American history.

Donald Smith, as governor of the HBC, met with Louis Riel and arranged for the Métis to negotiate directly with the Canadian government in 1870. Later, Smith was one of the partners in both the St. Paul, Minneapolis and Manitoba Railroad and the Canadian Pacific.

By the 1870s, the railroad boom was mostly over in Minnesota. Trains had crossed the state, first reaching the Red River at Breckenridge in 1871 and Moorhead just a few months later, but after that, railroad building seemed to stall once more. One of the Northern Pacific's branch railroads, the St. Paul and Pacific, fell into receivership, apparently without hope of resuscitation. A massive debt was owed to bondholders in Holland, but because the money raised by the bond offering had largely gone as payment to the railroad's owners rather than to build track, there appeared to be little value in the railroad itself. There was no money left to pay creditors or bondholders and certainly nothing for stockholders.

Hill realized, though, that the line still offered potential riches. The track already constructed could be used as the beginning of a line to Red River rather than as a mere connection to the Northern Pacific, and the massive land grant that would come with the completion of the tracks would more than pay for building the rest of the railroad. Hill estimated that the troubled line was worth $18 million, but when the Dutch bondholders sent representatives to Minnesota to find out if the company could be salvaged, he saw to it that they went away with a negative impression, probably going so far as to have the railroad's books juggled unfavorably.

Hill and his associates negotiated with the bondholders in 1877 and finally closed a deal by writing a promissory note worth $1 million to be used as a down payment on a total price of $5 million, also to be paid later. So, without spending a penny up front, Hill and his friends took control of the railroad. They then manipulated it into a new company, with financing initially provided by the Bank of Montreal, and they ended up with a new railroad through Minnesota and the Red River Valley to Manitoba.

The new railroad became the St. Paul, Minneapolis and Manitoba Railroad, and in a matter of months, Hill and his associates reversed the poor management that had plagued construction of the old line. Hill rode the tracks regularly, overseeing work as he went. No expense seemed too trivial to escape his interest, no detail too small to warrant his attention. Once, as he was riding in his personal railroad car out to examine the work, the train got stuck in a giant snowdrift. Hill grabbed a shovel and went at the snow with an energy that set an example for his workers.

On another occasion, as Hill walked along inspecting a new section of track, he came across a shiny railroad spike forgotten at the side of the recently laid steel. Furious at the waste, Hill picked up the spike and headed back to the crew working a couple of miles to the west. When the fast-thinking foreman saw Hill coming, he hurried out to meet him. "Oh, thank goodness you found it, Mr. Hill," the foreman called. "I've had three men looking for that spike all afternoon."

Hill filled in the gaps needed to complete the connection of steel rails from St. Paul west to the Red River Valley, and he also saw to the upgrading of much of the existing track that had been poorly laid. When the upgrades were finished, he extended the railroad north, mile after mile, following the Red River downstream to the Manitoba border. And as he completed each new section of track, Hill and his associates took control of the land grants promised by the state for the work. Almost as soon as the railroad qualified for the first of the grants, Hill's company sold off a portion of the land and raised $13 million. That money alone made Hill and his partners fabulously wealthy, but his new railroad was just getting started. Within a few more years, the wealth of Hill and his associates multiplied several times over.

By the end of December 1879, Hill's rail line was essentially complete to Manitoba, and Winnipeg finally had a railroad connecting it to the outside world. Nobody needed to take the cart trains to St. Paul any longer. The railroad was faster and cheaper. Parts of the old trail might still be used for local traffic between the new towns that were growing up along Hill's railroad, but the Red River Trail was finished, petering out as railroad traffic scooped up the commerce of the region. (Coincidently, only a couple of months after the first train rolled north to Manitoba, the first steam engine rolled into Santa Fe, New Mexico, and with the arrival of that railroad, the old Santa Fe Trail, too, vanished as an important North American trade route.)

With the new railroad, homesteaders streamed into the northern Red River Valley, but Pierre Bottineau had anticipated the new settlements. Three years before, while Hill was busy putting together his railroad scheme, Bottineau led a group of French-speaking residents on the upper Mississippi in a long caravan of ox-carts along the Red River Trail, from Osseo to the area around the Old Crossing of the Red Lake River. After Bottineau brought the first settlers to the region, he went to Winnipeg, where he encouraged more French-speaking homesteaders to migrate to the area around his new town of Red Lake Falls.

Soon afterward, other homesteaders looking for land in the Red River Valley could go all the way to Winnipeg on the St. Paul, Minneapolis and Manitoba Railroad, but Hill and his associates weren't finished building railroads. After Manitoba and British Columbia joined the young Canadian nation, a transcontinental railroad was promised, but for nearly a decade afterward, nothing but piecemeal construction and large scale corruption took place. The government of John A. Macdonald had even been thrown out of office for a time because of the railroad scandals.

When the St. Paul, Minneapolis and Manitoba Railroad reached the Canadian border, Macdonald, back in office after another election, saw a new opportunity. He thought the men behind the new railroad along the Red River Trail had experience that might be useful for building a railroad across northern Ontario and the Rocky Mountains. And they were Canadians who could, perhaps, build a cross-Canada line where others had failed.

In just over a year, Hill, Stephen, Smith and Kittson, with several new associates, became part of the Canadian Pacific Railroad in 1881. The undertaking turned out to have more engineering challenges than anything the men had attempted during the construction of what had become known as the "Manitoba Road." But despite the problems, in less than five years, the last spike would be driven on the Canadian Pacific, giving Manitoba a connection not only to the railroad that followed the old Red River Trail to St. Paul but also to a new one that stretched from one side of Canada to the other.

Bottineau, on his farm at Red Lake Falls, was by this time in semi-retirement, his guiding days behind him, living close to a new railroad and the northern end of the trail where he'd spent so much of his life. He lived just a few miles from where he had once saved his wilderness mentor, Antoine LeCompte, from the icy Red Lake River. He had traveled the nearby trail over and over again during the course of his life.

But in 1876, when Bottineau returned to the Red River Valley to live with his family, the old life of the Métis had mostly disappeared. The invasion of homesteaders into that part of northwestern Minnesota was only a recent chapter of a vanishing lifestyle. Aboriginal claims to almost all of the land south of the international boundary had been extinguished. The Métis population in Manitoba had already started to be overwhelmed with Canadian immigrants from Ontario and eastern Canada, to be followed by others from around the world. Most of the buffalo were gone. Railroads were taking the place of the old Red River Trail.

Ironically, it had been Bottineau, himself, who had helped bring about many of these events. He had moved to the upper Mississippi as a young man, more than a decade before the first wave of new settlers arrived from the east, and he spent most of his working life at tasks that ultimately helped bring an end to the frontier that had sustained him. He led immigrants across the plains, helped open vast areas in the middle of the continent to traders, lumber companies and railroads, assisted the government in gaining title to Native lands—land that belonged to his mother's people, land that he and other members of his family would also claim with government-issued Métis scrip. He had to live out the final years of his life in the little that remained of the frontier he had known as a youth.

Chapter Nineteen

Following the Trail Today

Life would not always be easy for Pierre Bottineau, the aging homesteader at Red Lake Falls. Despite his many attempts at land speculation, he had missed making the real-estate fortune that came to others on the upper Mississippi. This was largely because of his trusting nature, profligate ways with money and tendency to go on to someplace new before more people moved in and pushed property values high enough to create fortunes. As St. Paul's early population increased, Bottineau grew restless and moved to St. Anthony. After a few years there, when more people began to arrive, he moved on to Bottineau Prairie at Osseo. When larger numbers of settlers eventually came to Osseo, and the area began producing chickens for the growing Twin Cities market, he moved back to the Red River Country of his youth.

It is worth noting that Bottineau's farm at Red Lake Falls was obtained under a provision of the 1863 treaty he had helped negotiate with the Ojibwa. The treaty gave title of the Red River Valley to the government but was amended to allow Métis relatives of the Ojibwa to claim land scrip that could be exchanged for a homestead anywhere within the boundaries of the territory ceded by the bands. Just like Métis who qualified for land scrip in Manitoba, Bottineau and other members of his family could make claims for homesteads in northwestern Minnesota.

Still, after a time at Red Lake Falls, the aging home-steader's financial problems grew worse. At one point, money would be so short his wife, Martha, sold her wedding ring so the family could buy flour. Still, Bottineau was an admired public figure. Prominent friends in St. Paul petitioned the United States Congress to provide the old guide with a small pension. James J. Hill came to Red Lake Falls to visit Bottineau several times, and he gave his aging comrade and his family lifetime passes on his railroad.

But Congress approved a pension of only $25 a month, not the $50 that was suggested in the petition, and in the end, Bottineau still relied on many of the traditional skills he had learned on the plains in an earlier era, the same wilderness skills that had sustained him in life more than anything he was able to garner from the civilization and settlement he helped bring about. After a few years, Bottineau moved from his farm to a new brick home he built on the edge of Red Lake Falls. He died in the summer of 1895, after falling ill while hunting moose along the Red Lake River.

Initially, Bottineau was buried in a little country cem-etery almost within sight of the Red River Trail, near where it crossed the Red Lake River. Then, more than half a century later, after a local highway bypassed the tiny graveyard, leav-ing it stranded in a farmer's field, someone decided that Bot-tineau's body, along with other members of his family, should be moved to the cemetery at Red Lake Falls. Before the reburial, the Catholic priest overseeing the operation had the coffin opened, and he took a picture of the old guide's bones. Today, a sign at the cemetery notes Bottineau's burial there.

A decade ago, tracks from the original Red River carts could be found at the Old Crossing of the Red Lake River, near Bottineau's first gravesite. When I went back recently, I found they had been covered over by ruts dug by all-terrain vehicles. The trail, itself, drifted into history even before Bottineau passed away. Steam trains dominated North America's transportation system for a while, but as the 20th century unfolded, railroads became only part of the overall network of steel, highways and airways that connect people in today's world. Now there are modern highways on each side of the Red River, north and south of the international boundary, where the old trail used to be.

Some of these new roads more or less follow short stretches of the original trail. In other places wheat grows where unchecked winds once blew through the long, native prairie grasses. The frontier and the fur trade are gone, but there are a few spots on these plains where Pierre Bottineau and the long cart caravans can still be imagined. At areas along the old trail, it's possible to forget for a moment all the changes that have taken place since Bottineau was here, places where the changes seem almost trivial on the flat expanse of the still mostly treeless plains. Out in the country, on the open prairie, the sky still dominates the landscape, and the era of the Red River Trail—when the Ojibwa, Assiniboine and Sioux rode free and Métis cart trains snaked their way across the horizon—can still be imagined.

On the west side of the Red River, when I drive south through Manitoba and North Dakota, along the approximate route of the old West Plains Trail, the land, with only a few exceptions, appears unceasingly flat. Look beyond the road and the view might stretch uninterrupted for miles. It's a view often called "boring" by people from other places, by people who don't feel the exhilaration Pierre Bottineau found on the open plains. The immense sky and the distant horizons can be humbling, even overpowering, but they also evoke a feeling of emancipation, sometimes, I think, an exhilarating sense of pure liberty.

Even on the coldest days, when distant horizons seem closer and the frozen valley is topped by a deeper, bluer sky, and an orange sun is punctuated with sundogs, the vast openness of the plains gives birth to an invigorating and ever-renewing sense of freedom. It's the same feeling, I think, once felt by Natives of the plains, Métis buffalo hunters and 19th-century cowboys, all on horseback and riding free under these same prairie skies. It's what Pierre Bottineau must have felt traveling in the Red River Valley in the days when no towns, not even a homesteader's cabin, were to be found anywhere on the trail between Pembina and St. Paul.

Somewhat ironically, this immense sense of liberation in no way diminishes the harshness of the prairie landscape. Life can be exhilarating on the plains, but nothing arrives here with a sugar coating. In winter, snow and ice turn the prairie of the Red River Valley into what appears to be a giant, frozen lake. This land is huge and as hard and uncaring as when the March blizzard in 1837 blew suffering and death down on Pierre Bottineau and his companions.

No matter what the season, under the intense summer sun or the frozen skies of winter, it's an uncompromising landscape. Perhaps, the sense of liberation it imparts comes about because the openness and beauty of the plains are constantly tempered by nature's reality. Bottineau and other pilgrims on the Red River Trail found joy and freedom in equal measure with winter blizzards, spring rainstorms, floods, mosquitoes, oppressive summer heat and, sometimes, the rage of the prairie's native inhabitants.

Driving the route of the old trail today in a heated or air-conditioned car leaves a modern visitor somewhat shielded from the natural world, but even now, with all the changes that have come since Pierre Bottineau and the miles-long cart caravans passed this way, the prairie outside still seems connected to its past. At the end of a summer day not long ago, I stood on

Several road signs in Marshall County in northwestern Minnesota, like the one above, mark gravel roads where the Red River Trail used to be.

the open plains near Walhalla, North Dakota, outside the old trading post of Antoine Gingras who, like Bottineau, was a Red River Métis who spent much of his life on the trail.

Looking southeast, toward St. Paul, I imagined the view Bottineau would have seen so many years ago. Gingras' old trading post is barely three miles below the international boundary, only a few yards from what was once the Red River Trail, and it is now an official historic site, maintained by the North Dakota Historical Society. The buildings have been restored, but for me, standing outside, looking toward the Pembina River in the distance, the land I see has been transformed in ways that somehow make a lie of the buildings.

Most of what was once prairie is now a farmer's field. And the river, which once flowed by the buildings near where I stand, has shifted its course, moved by strong currents and erosion tumbling from the heights of the nearby hills. Even more distracting are the trees, in shelterbelts and woodlots that have grown up on the prairie since the time of roaming buffalo herds and raging prairie fires.

Despite the changes, perhaps because of the magic of the restored buildings and the shadow of the Pembina Mountains to the west, the Antoine Gingras Historic Site still stands out as one of the places I like best along the whole expanse of what was once the Red River Trail. Gingras started building the trading post here in 1843. A few years later, he built a separate house for his family. Today these buildings are the two oldest Euro-American buildings in North Dakota. Not far away, in a small park on the other side of town, is a cabin that Norman Kittson once used to store and trade furs. It might be the second oldest building in the state.

Louis Riel, when he fled from Manitoba after the 1870 uprising, came down the Red River Trail to this spot just over the border. He stayed with Antoine Gingras and his family. He worked in the trading post with Gingras for a while before moving on to Montana, and then Saskatchewan, where he staged one more failed fight with the Canadian Government and was hanged as a consequence.

Today, standing in the wind on the plains outside Gingras' old store, with the hills behind me and the memory of the trail nearby, I can look to the south and still imagine 19th-century Métis traders loading their carts before crossing the river and taking to the open country beyond. Afterward, I get in my car and drive a few miles away, then look back toward the old trading post and see the escarpment the Métis came to call the Pembina Mountains behind me on the horizon. I can imagine Pierre Bottineau somewhere along a nearby stretch of the Red River Trail looking back to see the same forested hills before turning once more to the long prairie trail going south to St. Paul.

The Native people and earliest traders of the region called the rugged, nearby escarpment the Hair Hills. Indian mounds, used hundreds, even thousands, of years ago for ceremonial purposes, are still found here and at other places nearby. Later, as the sun begins to set, I drive up into the hills and find something almost mystical in the fading light of the disappearing day. Stopped along a gravel road, looking into the shadows of a valley below, I realize that you do not need a religion to feel there would be spiritual stories about this place.

Following the old trail again, only a few minutes north of today's Grand Forks, the highway crosses Turtle River, probably just downriver from where Pierre Bottineau was born. A Métis wintering camp was used seasonally here for several years by the Bottineau family. For a time, the Hudson's Bay Company maintained a post nearby. Bottineau's father seems to have returned to the spot again and again during his life in the northwest.

The Métis were a nomadic people, and Charles Bottineau adopted that lifestyle for himself after he moved west. Some say he was one of the French Canadian traders who met with Lewis and Clark on the Missouri during their epic trek across the northern United States. An entry from Alexander Henry's journals in 1803 tells of the death of one of Charles' children at Pembina; another journal entry tells of a cart and pony trip between Pembina and the Hair Hills to go buffalo hunting. Yet another early report puts Charles near Rainy Lake, near today's International Falls, just a few months before his son Pierre was born.

More is known of Pierre Bottineau than of his father, but the details of his comings and goings on the Red River Trail are mostly missing, too. Nobody recorded his memories for publication the way people did for Kit Carson. We know that Bottineau was with Alexander Ramsey at Pembina in 1851. He was near Grand Forks, again helping to negotiate treaties with the Ojibwa in 1860. A little farther down the trail, he slipped through the Sioux lines around Fort Abercrombie and went for reinforcements to help the besieged soldiers during Minnesota's Sioux Uprising in 1862. Only a few years before that, he guided land speculators to Breckenridge, and he'd hoped to win real-estate riches of his own from a town that never came to be.

Driving south today, through the area where the old trail crossed the Red River in any number of spots before entering Minnesota—near Breckinridge, close to Georgetown, at Fort Abercrombie, along Route 27 on the east shore of Lake Traverse—you can retrace some of the old ox-cart trail. It's the route Pierre Bottineau took after the blizzard in 1837. There's a roadside marker near Georgetown commemorating the place where the Hudson's Bay Company set up shop to transfer goods from trail to steamboat. I've stopped at other places where placards mark fur company posts that once did business along the shores of Lake Traverse, at Big Stone Lake and Lac Qui Parle farther down the trail.

A few more miles to the south, the Minnesota Historical Society maintains a site near Redwood Falls, at the Lower Sioux Indian Reservation. Near St. Peter, the Nicollet County Historical Society runs a museum where traders established the trail community at Traverse de Sioux. It was here that the Sioux met to sign a peace treaty in 1851, and Norman Kittson brought his long cart trains from Pembina in the mid-1840s, even though most of the cart traffic had switched to the new, shorter branch of the trail through the lake country farther north. Outside the Traverse de Sioux museum, signposts mark places where buildings stood in the days when the trail first made the place an important stop in the Minnesota wilderness.

At the mouth of the Minnesota River, Fort Snelling has been restored just across the river from the similarly restored home of Henry Hastings Sibley, who built it when he ran the American Fur Company in the region. It was that site, in the shadow of the fort, which once provided early traders on the Red River Trail with an outlet for the furs they smuggled from the grasp of the Hudson's Bay Company.

Today, the walls of Fort Snelling are as impressive to visitors as they must have appeared to the Native people and new army recruits in the early 1820s. But now, platoons of soldiers dressed in 19th-century uniforms drill in the fort's yard for tourists, while nearby the sounds of the city—traffic on the freeways, planes landing at the Twin Cities Airport— seem to whine ceaselessly, making for a somewhat distorted interpretation of what life must have been like almost 200 years ago at the southern end of the Red River Trail.

Pierre Bottineau would have taken the trail along the Minnesota River Valley on his first visits to Fort Snelling, perhaps as early as 1830. In those years, he would have stayed with family members in one of the small log huts near the river below the fort, an old army barracks called Coldwater where people from Red River were first granted permission to stay. A few years later, he would have begun using the more direct Plains Trail across Minnesota, traveling from the Red River through the hills and lake country to the Mississippi.

By the 1840s, Bottineau had become one of St. Paul's pioneer settlers, owning land in what became the city's downtown, building a home and planting a small field of wheat somewhere near the corner of what is now Jackson and Seventh Street. But after a few years, he sold his holdings in St. Paul to move to a brand new settlement at St. Anthony

Falls. Going from downtown St. Paul today, past where the old trail passed near Bottineau's former property, the Red River Trail followed the approximate route of today's University Avenue. Near the Mississippi, not far from where Bottineau's St. Anthony home once stood, the trail would have swung north again, following the course of the river, approximately as far as today's Highway 10, where it would have turned in similar fashion to the west.

The Mississippi River as seen from a spot where the town of Crow Wing was once a stop on the Red River Trail. On the opposite shore, the mouth of the Crow Wing River is just to the south of the wing-shaped island for which it was named.

At St. Cloud, the Plains Trail crossed the Mississippi and angled northwest toward the Red River. For those who want to follow the Crow Wing branch of the trail today, it is best done by staying on Highway 10, on the east side of the Mississippi, continuing north past Little Falls to State Highway 371 and then following that road north to Crow Wing State Park.

Just like visitors at Traverse de Sioux, those at Crow Wing, today, can walk through a well-marked, but now vanished, village. Small signs mark spots where stores and homes once stood. Only an old mission church remains of the former settlement. At one time, the town could have boasted several hundred residents. Today, there isn't even a bridge over what is, so far north, the narrow Mississippi. You have to drive farther north to find a way across the river if you are trying to retrace the path of the old trail. You can, however, see the spot where the ferry landed above the old town in the mid-19th century, and you can walk a trail along the Mississippi through what was once a thriving frontier settlement.

On the opposite side of the river, between the Crow Wing's two outlets on the Mississippi, lies the island whose shape gives the smaller river its name. A few miles beyond, on the north side of the Crow Wing River, you can cross Pillager Creek, at the town of Pillager, where a band of Ojibwa once had a run-in with a trader and were tagged, probably unfairly, with the disparaging name.

After Pillager, the old path of the trail can rejoin Highway 10 at Motley. Farther on, a slight detour leads from the highway to Old Wadena, another ghost town, now a county park, where the original Wadena was built on the trail near the mouth of the Leaf River. The earliest people to come through here on the trail thought the Leaf was a continuation of the Crow Wing, assuming the upstream stretch of today's Crow Wing River was a mere tributary to a larger stream.

The site near the confluence of the Leaf and Crow Wing rivers had been used, occasionally, by traders beginning in the late 1700s. A little more than a decade after the Woods Trail was added as a branch of the Red River Trail in 1844, the first homesteader arrived. His name was Augustus Aspinwall,

The display board at Crow Wing State Park tells the story of the Woods Trail, the eastern branch of the Red River Trail.

FOLLOWING THE TRAIL TODAY

and he was so sure the spot he called Wadena would one day become a thriving community that he plotted city roads and surveyed house lots to sell when the throngs of people arrived.

Aspinwall was too early to create a boomtown (he moved to the area just before the Panic of 1857), and folks on the Red River Trail sometimes noted, somewhat cynically, that there was only one log cabin in the "town" of Wadena. Later, a few settlers did arrive, but a new railroad soon passed the community by and everyone moved away, many to the new railroad town also called Wadena a few miles away on today's Highway 10.

Following the old trail west along the Leaf River, past the spot where Aspinwall's cabin had been, took earlier visitors through the low hills known as the Leaf Mountains, which mark the divide between the Arctic and Atlantic watersheds. At Ottertail Lake, another marker notes the earlier trail, as does yet another sign at Detroit Lakes, near where the trail came out of the forested hills to cross the prairies (or depending on the direction of travel, left the prairies to go into the forested hills).

No matter what branch of the trail was used, the meeting place of prairie and gently rolling forest on the eastern side of the Red River Valley made for a distinct dividing point in the 19th century on the Red River Trail. Even if the distance between starting and ending points wasn't exactly halfway on each side of this divide, the marked change in landscape was a telling feature when going to or from the upper Mississippi. It was a point where, near the Continental Divide, the landscape made an abrupt change, where the journey became something different than it had been before, where an essentially flat plain became rolling, where forests extended to the prairies and water ultimately ran south instead of north.

On the original route, travelers beyond Lake Traverse, at the Red River's headwaters, left the old lakebed of the valley behind, exchanging it in a few more miles for the deeper, truer valley of the Minnesota River. On the Plains Trail to St. Cloud, the landscape turned from open prairie to the glacially formed lakes and hills of northwestern Minnesota, much as it did farther north where the trail crossed from the Arctic watershed on the Woods Trail to the Atlantic watershed of the Gulf of Mexico beyond the Otter Tail River.

For Pierre Bottineau and others coming from the north, there must have been a symbolic moment at these points where they suddenly came upon a new and different country, from the prairie to the forest, from the liberation of the plains, perhaps, to the protection of the trees. The change would have been much more noticeable than merely crossing the consistently prairie landscape at the international boundary. It was an unmistakable change in geography, and one would suppose, one of psychology as well. It was where people left the Great Plains and entered the gently undulating forests on the way to St. Paul, with all its connections to the east and civilization.

In 1876, when Bottineau led more than 100 settlers in the opposite direction, he took people from what had been their homes on the upper Mississippi back to the plains. These mostly Métis homesteaders, bolstered two years later by others who came south to Red Lake Falls from Manitoba, became part of Minnesota's new agricultural frontier. But these settlers were different than most of the others who came later.

These homesteaders didn't come to a new frontier community just to establish farms and homes. They were former residents, like Pierre Bottineau, or the sons and daughters of former residents, who in a sense were returning to their prairie heritage, to the freedom of the plains, to regain what they could of their old life along the Red River Trail. Soon, settlers from other places would also fill the empty places across northwestern Minnesota, North Dakota, Manitoba and beyond to places farther west.

My home is about 90 miles north of Bottineau's old home at Red Lake Falls. Cart caravans going south from Fort Garry were only a couple of days on the trail when they went by what one day would become my land, land my wife and I will own for almost no time at all in the grand scheme of things. We don't even know the old trail's exact location, though we can guess about where it crossed nearby rivers and creeks along the way.

The trail must have crossed the Roseau River three miles south of our house, at one of two fords where the river is shallow and the banks are low. The best guess is that it crossed at a spot on the river where the Ojibwa built a fishing weir that was still in use when white settlers came to this area. On the little creek near where I live, some areas are more likely to have been crossing places than others. Link the crossing points on rivers and streams, follow the ridges where conditions of travel would have been easiest, and you can draw a pretty good map of where the old trail might have been.

Today, the tree line at the edge of the plains lies along a highway at the end of the two-mile gravel road that stretches west from my house, but nobody can be sure exactly where the trees started and the prairie ended at the time of the Woods Trail. Before western settlement by whites, the eastern edge of the plains varied from year to year. The forest edge usually lay farther east than it does today, but the line between plains and woodland changed, depending on drought and fire. In drought years, fires burned farther east; in wet years, hazel nuts and poplar trees reclaimed more of the western prairie for the forest.

The border between east and west, where woods and prairie meet, has always been a jagged, north-south line that changed from place to place and year to year. The route of the Red River Trail varied, too, for any number of reasons. In the 1840s, well before the first agricultural settlers arrived in this area, the tree line between east and west could easily have been as close as the yard where my house stands today, or even farther east than that. No one knows because the dividing line between woods and prairie was never a static position. Today, we know the old cart trail would have been somewhere on these beach ridges, instead of the often wet prairie just to the west, but exactly where is hard, perhaps impossible, to determine.

More than a century has passed since any of those carts crossed the valley and tiny creek that runs through my ranch. Documents at a government office show that the first owners of this property were named Ouellette, and like Pierre Bottineau, they obtained their land with Métis scrip. They held title to the land only a short time, which makes me suspect that, like so many other Métis, they lost the property the government said was supposed to repay them for the land, and freedom, they had given up. For most Métis, no real sense of repatriation ever took place.

All this, of course, was long ago. Clear tracks marking the old pathway have disappeared at this place as completely as the Ouellettes. Still, geologic time is different than it is for short-lived human beings. The earth shifts, erodes, covers itself and evolves in a variety of ways and speeds. There could still be clues to those times left here to be found. For the land, Pierre Bottineau and the twisting cart trains, grinding and screeching along the trail south to the Mississippi, passed by this place only a moment ago.

After his death in 1895, an obituary in the *St. Paul Pioneer* called Pierre Bottineau the Kit Carson of the North. It was a comparison that had been used before and would be used afterward, even though it came with all the shortcomings such comparisons generally exhibit. The one thing that's true is that when the Red River Trail ceased to exist, when trains and automobiles replaced the old Red River carts, when people like Pierre Bottineau, Kit Carson and others passed on, a peculiar and colorful era came to an end in the North American West.

It is ironic that both Carson and Bottineau did so much to further the changes that ended the frontier where they had thrived. They lived in a world that vanished with the arrival of railroads and homesteaders, leaving them in a new world that they helped create but were unsuited to live in. Over their lifetimes, the buffalo hunt and fur trade gave way to ranchers and homesteaders; the great wilderness of the plains turned to settlement and civilization. The trails they knew disappeared, and nobody ever went down them again.

Timeline

1797: Pierre Bottineau's father, Charles, comes west as an employee of the North West Company.

1805: Zebulon Pike explores the upper Mississippi for the United States and signs a treaty with Sioux to allow the army to build a fort at the confluence of the Mississippi and Minnesota rivers.

1812: First Selkirk Settlers arrive at forks of Red and Assiniboine rivers and buy potatoes and produce from Charles Bottineau. War of 1812 begins between Britain and the United States; lasts for two years.

1816: Battle of Seven Oaks.

1817: Pierre Bottineau is born to Canadian Charles Joseph Bottineau and Marguerite Ahdik Songab (Clear Sky), an Ojibwa, at a winter camp near what would become known as the Red River Trail.

Thomas Douglas, the 5th Earl of Selkirk, visits Red River and follows the Red River Trail to the Mississippi, where he continues to the United States east coast before returning to Europe.

Captain Stephen H. Long makes his first expedition to the upper Mississippi, recommends building a fort at the confluence of Mississippi and Minnesota rivers where Zebulon Pike had already suggested.

1818: Britain and the United States agree to an international boundary across the North American plains at the 49th parallel.

1820: Construction of Fort Snelling begins.

Thomas Douglas dies in Europe.

1821: The Hudson's Bay Company merges with the North West Company. Nicholas Garry comes from London to oversee the reorganization of the two companies into the HBC.

Michael Dousman attempts to take cattle to Red River, but Dakota kill the herd at Lake Traverse.

The Columbia Fur Company is founded.

1822: First settlers arrive at Fort Snelling from Red River.

1823: Stephen Long returns to the upper Mississippi with an expedition that documents the Red River Trail for the first time and marks the international border near Pembina.

1824: Fort Snelling is completed.

1827: American Fur Company buys out Columbia Fur Company.

Hudson's Bay Company governor George Simpson marries his cousin Frances Simpson.

1830: Pierre Bottineau probably makes first trip to the upper Mississippi about this time.

1836: Pierrie Bottineau marries Genevieve LaRonce at Red River.

1837: Bottineau is caught on the Red River Trail with Martin McCleod during a great March blizzard.

1838: Bottineau takes cattle, furs and immigrants down the trail to the upper Mississippi.

1839: Métis trader James Sinclair takes the largest ox-cart train of its time to the American Fur Company at Mendota.

1840: Antoine LeCompte is killed by Thomas Simpson, who dies on the trail at his own hand.

A large buffalo hunt with 1600 Métis and more than 1200 Red River carts takes place.

Bottineau is evicted from his cabin on military land on the east side of the Mississippi along with Pig's Eye Parrant and others. Bottineau takes another claim inside what would become the city of St. Paul.

1844: The Woods branch of the Red River Trail is built through Crow Wing to Red River.

Norman Kittson takes over the American Fur Company post at Pembina.

Louis Riel is born at Red River.

1845: Bottineau buys land at St. Anthony Falls.

1846: British troops arrive at Red River and stay two years.

1849: Free-trade trial convicts four Métis men but imposes no penalties. The Hudson's Bay Company monopoly is essentially abolished.

James Sinclair returns to Red River country from California gold rush.

Pierre Bottineau buys an inn and trading post at Elk River.

1850: Bottineau builds another inn and trading post a short distance away from Elk River.

1851: Pierre Bottineau's wife, Genevieve, dies in April at their home near the Falls of St. Anthony.

A treaty is signed with the Sioux in Minnesota but amended by United States Senate to take away most of their Minnesota River Valley homeland.

Bottineau guides Territorial Governor Alexander Ramsey to Pembina to negotiate a treaty with Ojibwa, but the Senate later rejects the treaty.

1852: In January, Bottineau marries Martha Gervais. Including this marriage, after his first wife's death in 1851, Bottineau fathers 26 children, several of whom fail to survive childhood.

1853: Bottineau guides Isaac Stevens, carrying out the first Northern Pacific Railroad survey across the northern United States. In the fall, he guides a group of English bankers on a hunting trip on the Red River Trail.

1854: Bottineau files a claim at what became known as "Bottineau Prairie" near today's Osseo, Minnesota.

1855: James Sinclair is killed in a Native uprising in Oregon.

1856: Bottineau guides soldiers looking for sites for forts west of the Red River.

1857: Bottineau leads land speculators to the Red River at today's Breckenridge, Minnesota.

The Panic of 1857 begins an economic depression that impedes development in Minnesota until after the Civil War.

1859: The first steamboat, the *Anson Northrup*, used on the Red River arrives in Winnipeg.

James Carnegie, the Earl of Southesk, travels in May with Hudson's Bay governor George Simpson between Crow Wing and Winnipeg.

Robert Mackenzie, manager of the Hudson's Bay Company at Georgetown, freezes to death on the Red River Trail at the end of December while trying to reach Pembina.

1860: Bottineau guides treaty delegations to meet with several Ojibwa bands from northern Minnesota

1861: American Civil War begins.

1862: Bottineau leads wagon train west to Montana.

The Sioux uprising begins in August. Bottineau slips through the Sioux siege around Fort Abercrombie to go for help. Thirty-nine Sioux leaders are hanged at Mankato, Minnesota, in late December in the largest mass execution in American history.

1863: Little Crow is shot and killed near Hutchinson, Minnesota.

Bottineau leads American troops west to the Missouri River searching for the last of those involved in the Sioux uprising. When he returns, he travels to Pembina with a treaty delegation to help in negotiations that result in the Ojibwa giving up their claim to most of northwestern Minnesota, including large portions of the Red River Trail.

1865: Civil War ends.

Medicine Bottle and Shakopee are hanged at Fort Snelling after being kidnapped by local residents at Red River and turned over to American authorities at nearby Pembina.

1867: Bottineau leads Captain A.H. Terry into Dakota Territory to build Fort Ransom.

1869: Canadian government purchases western Canada from Hudson's Bay Company.

Louis Riel leads Métis in Red River Rebellion and forms a provisional government in December.

Bottineau guides route for second Northern Pacific Railroad survey.

1870: The Manitoba Act makes Manitoba Canada's first western province.

Bottineau guides James J. Hill on his return from Red River to St. Paul.

1872: Official boundary between Canada and the United States places Pembina in United States. Sometime later, Jud LaMoure wins land where Pembina sits today, in a poker game.

1876: Bottineau leads more than 100 families from the upper Mississippi to settle in the Red River Valley in northwestern Minnesota. Two years later, he brings more settlers from Manitoba.

1879: James J. Hill's St. Paul, Minneapolis and Manitoba Railroad reaches Manitoba, giving Winnipeg a rail link to the south.

1895: Pierrie Bottineau dies at Red Lake Falls.

Notes on Sources

Introduction

Coffin, Charles Carleton. *Seat of Empire*. Boston: Fields, Osgood & Co., 1870.

Connolly, A.P. *Minnesota Massacre and the Sioux War of 1862–63*, published by the author, Chicago, 1896.

Sides, Hampton. *Blood and Thunder: An Epic of the American West*. New York: Doubleday, 2006.

Chapter 1: The Blizzard

Newman, Peter C. *Caesars of the Wilderness, Volume II, Company of Adventurers*. Toronto: Viking Penguin Books, 1987.

Nute, Grace Lee. "James Dickson: A Filibuster in Minnesota in 1836." *Mississippi Valley Historical Review*, X, Sept. 1923.

Nute, Grace Lee. *McLeod's Diary, Minnesota History*. Minnesota Historical Society, Vol. 4. Aug.–Nov. 1922. (An article in Minnesota Historical Society Scrapbook, Vol. 2, p. 94, at the Minnesota Historical Society Archives could also be of interest.)

Chapter 2: The Trail

Gilman, Rhoda R, Carolyn Gilman, and Deborah Stultz. *The Red River Trails: Oxcart Routes Between St. Paul and the Selkirk Settlement, 1820–1870*. St. Paul: Minnesota Historical Society Press, 1979.

MacEwan, Grant. *Blazing the Old Cattle Trail*. Saskatoon: Modern Press, 1962.

Morton, W.L., *Manitoba: A History*. Toronto: University of Toronto Press, 1957.

Newman, Peter C. *Caesars of the Wilderness, Volume II, Company of Adventurers*. Toronto: Viking Penguin Books, 1987.

Chapter 3: The Métis

Brehaut, Harry B. *The Red River Cart and Trail*. Scientific Society of Manitoba, papers, Series 3, Vol. 28, Winnipeg, 1971–72.

Fonseca, William G. *On the St. Paul Trail in the '60s.* Manitoba Historical Society, Transactions Series 1, No. 56, January 1900.

Garrioch, Peter. Diary manuscript. Winnipeg: Manitoba Provincial Archives.

Giraud, Marcel. *The Métis in the Canadian West, Volumes 1 and 2.* Translated by George Woodcock. Edmonton: University of Alberta Press, 1986.

Havard, V., United States Assistant Surgeon. *The French Half-Breeds of the Northwest.* Smithsonian Annual Report, Washington, 1879.

Henry, Alexander. *The Manuscript Journals of Alexander Henry, Vol. 1.* Edited by Elliott Coues. NY: Francis P. Harper, 1897.

Howard, Joseph Kinsey. *The Strange Empire of Louis Riel.* NY: William Morrow & Co., 1952.

Newman, *Caesars of the Wilderness.*

Ross, Alexander. *The Red River Settlement: Its Rise, Progress and Present State,* London, Smith, Elder & Company, 1856.

Chapter 4: Red River
Giraud, *The Métis in the Canadian West.*

Newman, *Caesars of the Wilderness.*

Halkett, John. *Statement Respecting the Earl of Selkirk's Settlement in North America.* London: John Murray, 1817.

Howard, *The Strange Empire.*

Pritchett, John P."A Letter by Lord Selkirk on Trade Between Red River and the United States." *Canadian Historical Review,* Vol. 17, 418–23, December 1936.

Chapter 5: The Upper Mississippi
Adams, Ann. (transcribed by J. Fletcher Williams). *Mrs. Adams' Reminiscences of Red River and Fort Snelling.* Minnesota Historical Collections, Vol. 6., 75–116. St. Paul: Minnesota Historical Society and Pioneer Press Co., 1894.

Jones, Evan. *Citadel in the Wilderness: The Story of Fort Snelling and the Northwest Frontier.* Minneapolis: University of Minnesota Press, 1966.

Taliaferro, Lawrence. Autobiography, Minnesota Historical Collections, Vol. 6, Pioneer Press Company, 1894, St. Paul. See also: Taliaferro papers Minnesota Historical Society Archives.

Chapter 6: The Soldiers and the Count

Cavileer, Charles Turner. *A Red River Journey in 1851.* University of North Dakota Library Special Collections, Speech given in Grand Forks, North Dakota, December 10, 1891.

Giraud, *The Métis in the Canadian West.*

Keating, William H. *Narrative of an Expedition to the Source of the St. Peter's River in the Year 1823, Vol. 1 and 2,* George Whittaker, London, 1925; also Ross & Haines, Minneapolis, 1959.

Long, Stephen H. *The Northern Expeditions of Stephen H. Long: The Journals of 1817 and 1823 and Related Documents,* edited by Lucile Kane, June Holmquist and Carolyn Gilman. St. Paul: Minnesota Historical Society Press, 1978.

McCullough, David. *Mornings on Horseback.* NY: Simon & Schuster, 1981.

Powers, Thomas. *The Killing of Crazy Horse.* New York: Random House, 2010.

Chapter 7: The Fur Companies

Barbour, Barton H. Fort Union and the Upper Missouri Fur Trade. Norman, OK: University of Oklahoma Press, 2001.

Giraud, *The Métis in the Canadian West.*

Lavender, David. *A Fist in the Wilderness.* Garden City, NY: Doubleday, 1964.

Chapter 8: Smuggling on the Red River Trail

Garrioch, Diary manuscript.

Gluek, Alvin C. Jr. *Minnesota and the Manifest Destiny of the Canadian Northwest.* Toronto: University of Toronto Press, 1965.

Klassen, Henry Cornelius. *The Red River Settlement and the St. Paul Route, 1859–1870.* Master's thesis, Department of History, University of Manitoba, Winnipeg, 1963.

Lent, Geneva. *West of the Mountains: James Sinclair and the Hudson's Bay Company*. Seattle: University of Washington Press, 1963.

Newman, *Caesars of the Wilderness*.

Thompson, Albert Edward. *Chief Peguis and his Descendants*. Winnipeg: Peguis Publishers, 1973.

Chapter 9: On the Trail with Pierre Bottineau

Bray, Martha. "Pierre Bottineau: Professional Guide," *North Dakota Quarterly*, Spring 1964, Vol. 32, 29–37.

Giraud, *The Métis in the Canadian West*.

Jorgenson, Margareth. *The Life of Pierre Bottineau*. Unpublished manuscript, 1925, found in Minnesota Historical Society Archives, St. Paul.

Simpson, Alexander. *The Life and Travels of Thomas Simpson: The Arctic Discoverer*. London: Richard Bentley, 1845.

Stevenson, John A. "The Unsolved Death of Thomas Simpson," *The Beaver*, June 1935.

Williams, John Fletcher. *A History of the City of St. Paul and the County of Ramsey, Minnesota*. St. Paul: Minnesota Historical Society, 1876.

Chapter 10: Crow Wing

Carnegie, James (Earl of Southesk). *Saskatchewan and the Rocky Mountains: A Diary of Travel, Sport & Adventure During a Journey Through the Hudson's Bay Company's Territory in 1859 and 1860*. Edinburgh: Edmonston & Douglas, 1875.

Garrioch, Diary manuscript.

Lent, Geneva. *West of the Mountains: James Sinclair and the Hudson's Bay Company*. Seattle: University of Washington Press, 1963.

MacEwan, Grant. *Métis: Makers of History*. Saskatoon: Western Producer Prairie Books, 1981.

Warren, William W. *History of the Ojibway People*. St. Paul: Minnesota Historical Society Press, 1984.

Chapter 11: Pembina

Cavileer, *A Red River Journey in 1851*.

Gilman, Rhoda R, Carolyn Gilman, and Deborah Stultz. *The Red River Trails: Oxcart Routes Between St. Paul and the Selkirk Settlement, 1820–1870*. St. Paul: Minnesota Historical Society Press, 1979.

Henry, Alexander. *The Manuscript Journals of Alexander Henry, Vol. 1*. Edited by Elliott Coues. NY: Francis P. Harper, 1897.

Garrioch, Diary manuscript.

Lee, Charles. *The Long Ago: A Collection of Historic Anecdotes of Early Days in the Valley of the Red River of the North*. Walhalla, ND: Weekly Mountaineer Press, 1899.

Rees, Tony, *The Arc of the Medicine Line: Mapping the World's Longest Undefended Border Across the Western Plains*, University of Nebraska Press, Lincoln, 2008.

Chapter 12: Pig's Eye Parrant and the Founding of St. Paul

Federal Writers Project, Works Progress Administration. *The WPA Guide to Minnesota*. St. Paul: Minnesota Historical Society Press, 1985.

Gluek, *Minnesota and the Manifest Destiny*.

Taliaferro, Autobiography.

Williams, John Fletcher. *A History of the City of St. Paul and the County of Ramsey, Minnesota*. St. Paul: Minnesota Historical Society, 1876.

Chapter 13: The Trail to St. Paul

Garrioch, Diary manuscript.

Gilman, Rhoda R, Carolyn Gilman, and Deborah Stultz. *The Red River Trails: Oxcart Routes Between St. Paul and the Selkirk Settlement, 1820–1870*. St. Paul: Minnesota Historical Society Press, 1979.

Gluek, *Minnesota and the Manifest Destiny*.

MacEwan, Grant. *Blazing the Old Cattle Trail*. Saskatoon: Modern Press, 1962.

Morris, Lucy (ed.) *Old Rail Fence Corners*. St. Paul: Minnesota Historical Society Press, 1974.

Chapter 14: James Sinclair and Free Trade

Howard, *The Strange Empire*.

Lent, Geneva. *West of the Mountains: James Sinclair and the Hudson's Bay Company*. Seattle: University of Washington Press, 1963.

Newman, *Caesars of the Wilderness*.

Chapter 15: Minnesota Statehood

Babcock, Willoughby M. "With Ramsey to Pembina: A Treaty-Making Trip in 1851." *Minnesota History Magazine,* St. Paul, MN, March 1962.

Federal Writers Project, *The WPA Guide to Minnesota*.

Gluek, *Minnesota and the Manifest Destiny*.

Haldberg, Jane. *The Story of Pierre Bottineau*. Brooklyn, NY: Brooklyn Historical Society, 1979.

Johnston, Daniel S.B. *A Red River Townsite Speculation in 1857*. Collections of the Minnesota Historical Society, St. Paul, XV.

Kaplan, Anne, and Marilyn Ziebarth (eds.) *Making Minnesota Territory 1849–1858*. St. Paul: Minnesota Historical Society Press, 1999.

Scudder, S.H. *The Winnipeg Country, or Roughing it with an Eclipse Party*. Boston: Rand, Avery & Co., 1886.

Chapter 16: Let Them Eat Grass

Adams, *Mrs. Adams' Reminiscence*.

Coffin, *Seat of Empire*.

Corcoran, John. *Diary, Bulletin of the Missouri Historical Society*. April 1957.

Giraud, *The Métis in the Canadian West*.

Gluek, *Minnesota and the Manifest Destiny*.

Hawkinson, Ella. "The Old Crossing Chippewa Treaty and Its Sequel." *Minnesota History,* Vol. 15, Sept. 1934.

Jones, Evan. *The Minnesota*. Minneapolis: University of Minnesota Press, 1962.

Keating, *Narrative of an Expedition*.

Morton, W.L., *Battle at the Grand Coteau: Historical Essays on the Prairie Provinces*. Edited by Donald Swainson. Toronto: McClelland & Stewart, 1970.

Schultz, Duane P. *Over the Earth I Come: The Great Sioux Uprising of 1862.* New York: St. Martin's Press, 1992.

Meyer, Roy, "The Canadian Sioux: Refugees from Minnesota," *Minnesota History Magazine,* Spring, St. Paul, 1968.

Chapter 17: A New Province

Albro, Martin. *James J. Hill and the Opening of the Northwest.* New York: Oxford University Press, 1976.

Gilman, Carolyn. "Perceptions of the Prairie: Cultural Contrasts on the Red River Trails." *Minnesota History Magazine,* Fall 1978.

Gluek, *Minnesota and the Manifest Destiny.*

Langford, Nathaniel P. *Diary of 1870 Travel to Red River, Langford Papers.* St. Paul: Minnesota Historical Society Collection.

Morton, W.L. (ed.). *Alexander Begg's Red River Journal and Other Papers Relative to the Red River Resistance of 1869–70.* Toronto: Champlain Society, 1956.

Schultz, *Over the Earth I Come.*

Chapter 18: Red River by Rail

Albro, *James J. Hill.*

Bodkin, B.A., *Treasury of Railroad Folklore.* New York: Crown Publishers, 1953.

Berton, Pierre. *The National Dream: The Great Railway 1871–1881.* Toronto: McClelland and Stewart, 1970.

Gluek, *Minnesota and the Manifest Destiny.*

LaDow, Beth. *The Medicine Line: Life and Death on a North American Borderland.* New York and London: Routledge, 2002.

Chapter 19: Following the Trail Today

Gilman, Gilman and Stultz. *The Red River Trails.*

Jones, Evan. *The Minnesota.* Minneapolis: University of Minnesota Press, 1962.

Kaplan and Ziebarth. *Making Minnesota Territory.*

Ted Stone

Ted Stone has been a writer and editor for newspapers, magazines and book publishers in the United States and Canada for more than 30 years. He has taught journalism, creative writing and storytelling courses, and he has performed as a storyteller or public speaker at a variety of venues, including the Fort Edmonton Storytelling Festival and the Yukon International Storytelling Festival.

He has more than a dozen books to his credit, one of which was short-listed for the Stephen Leacock Memorial Medal for Humour. He lives on a ranch in southeastern Manitoba where he writes and looks after horses, and the path that was once the Red River Trail is nearby.